# Elemental
# Divination

## About the Author

Stephen Ball has been involved with magical practice and religion for over twenty years, working in Druidry, Shamanism, and initiatory Wicca in the UK. He has previously published *The Apple Branch: An English Shamanism* and contributed to the Neopagan anthology *Horns of Power* (as Stephen Blake). He has taught workshops on divination systems and a correspondence course on Shamanism. Stephen lives in London.

# Elemental Divination

## A DICE ORACLE

STEPHEN BALL

Llewellyn Publications
Woodbury, Minnesota

FIRST EDITION
Third Printing, 2021

Book design by Bob Gaul
Cover design by Shira Atakpu
Interior dice readings by Llewellyn art department

Llewellyn Publications is a registered trademark of Llewellyn Worldwide Ltd.

**Library of Congress Cataloging-in-Publication Data**
Names: Ball, Stephen.
Title: Elemental divination: a dice oracle / Stephen Ball.
Description: First edition. | Woodbury, Minnesota: Llewellyn Publications,
    [2018] | Includes bibliographical references.
Identifiers: LCCN 2017046408 (print) | LCCN 2017056388 (ebook) | ISBN
    9780738755748 (ebook) | ISBN 9780738754475 (alk. paper)
Subjects: LCSH: Fortune-telling by dice. | Oracles. | Divination.
Classification: LCC BF1891.D5 (ebook) | LCC BF1891.D5 B35 2018 (print) | DDC
    133.3—dc23
LC record available at https://lccn.loc.gov/2017046408

Llewellyn Worldwide Ltd. does not participate in, endorse, or have any authority or responsibility concerning private business transactions between our authors and the public.

All mail addressed to the author is forwarded but the publisher cannot, unless specifically instructed by the author, give out an address or phone number.

Any Internet references contained in this work are current at publication time, but the publisher cannot guarantee that a specific location will continue to be maintained. Please refer to the publisher's website for links to authors' websites and other sources.

Llewellyn Publications,
a Division of Llewellyn Worldwide Ltd.
2143 Wooddale Drive
Woodbury, MN 55125-2989
www.llewellyn.com
Printed in the United States of America

*To Emily, who already knew the way.*

# Contents

# Introduction

FOR ALMOST 2500 years, scholars have used the four elements to symbolize the primal forces of nature. Ideas from ancient Greece inspired many systems through the centuries and grew to be important tools for philosophers, magicians, alchemists, and early scientists around the world.

Along the way, Earth, Air, Fire, and Water have become associated with all the details of human life: emotions, intelligence, protection, wealth, freedom, love, and security. They can combine to represent the concerns and challenges facing everyone.

This oracle takes these fundamental forces and reads the pattern created by their play together. As we feel their heat in our blood and body or see the power of a moonlit storm over the sea, these readings draw on shared experiences that the elements give to all.

The structure of the oracle is simple, but the scenarios it reveals are deep and complex. I've used and created many divination systems over the years, but I realized I'd begun to leave them aside entirely in favor of rolling the dice to generate these beautiful images—The Waking Dreamer, Diamonds in the Stream, The Dragon's Breath.

Added to the classic four elements are two more symbols that have earned an equally important place in magical systems: the Sun and the Moon. These have always been powerfully present in people's lives and imaginations, and have long magical associations with science, magic, success, and mystery.

In this book you will find information on the elements and their associations in divination, instructions and rituals for using the oracle, and a list of definitions for each combination. You can take these meanings as the whole answer, or (if you are confident with the typical magical correspondences of the elements from another system, such as the tarot) you can use each combination as the starting point for a wider range of your own interpretations.

I hope that this oracle inspires readers to a deeper connection with the elements in magic, in our own bodies and around us in nature.

## The Structure of the Oracle

The oracle shows two elements meeting. One is the current situation, and the other is a newcomer that is either stronger or weaker. In the many permutations that result from these pairings, the struggles and delights of human life can be seen.

Three dice are rolled, with a number assigned to each element. This book lists the meanings and images of all the combinations of these rolls with a commentary on each. This method of rolling dice and consulting a book is in fact very old, and it uses the magical correspondences of each element to bring forth all the rich and colorful possibilities of a classical oracle.

## The Use of Dice in Divination

Dice have existed for thousands of years and they have been used in oracular work for most of that time. When we say the word *oracle*, many people think of the famous Oracle at Delphi: a person receiving messages while in a trance. However, just as common as trance oracles were those involving dice, and Delphi itself was also a site for this type of divination!

Dice made from animal bones, known as astragaloi, were a major oracle in ancient Greece. For example, Pausanias says that there was a statue of Hercules in a grotto in Achaia (an area to the West of Athens) where these astragaloi dice were rolled and the answer was then looked up in a book. They have also been found next to an altar to Aphrodite in Athens and at several other major sites. Dice were also common in Rome. Soon imitation "bones" were being made from wood, glass, bronze, and ivory.

This format of dice oracles being paired with a text is evidenced around the world over many centuries. Texts such as the *Greek Magical Papyri* give a system for rolling three six-sided dice (or one die three times) and then finding the appropriate page for the meaning. The elemental oracle is cast in a very similar way.

Alongside divination, dice were also used for gambling and in children's games. Even in those games they often retained their early magical significance—nonreligious dice games in Greece in later years still included the names of gods. As objects, the linking of dice with magic and religion goes back in history much farther and early primitive dice (which were deliberately shaped like animal bones) were found in Tutankhamun's tomb, dated to 1333 BCE. Moving to more recent times, the late medieval era in Europe saw a huge resurgence of using dice to choose oracle entries from a book.

So while modern magicians often think of tarot cards as an obvious tool for divination, dice also have a long and important history in predicting the future and seeking answers from the powerful forces in nature.

## The History of Using Correspondences with the Elements

Many magical systems use "correspondences" to link the elements to aspects of human life. This works from the idea that forces and objects are connected in a way that isn't physical, that having an effect on one of the pair can cause changes to the one that it is linked to as well.

This is known as "sympathetic magic." Although that name wasn't used until the 1800s, it describes a system that had existed in some cultures before recorded history: the most famous example of this activity is of someone making a figure or doll to resemble their enemy and then attacking the doll in the hope that similar attacks will happen to the person. Other methods include associating plants, animals, and gods with illnesses due to their color, properties, or even their shape.

We have many written documents showing how sympathetic magic grew over the centuries and how the correspondences as we know them today were gathered. An important early start came again from ancient Greece, where Empedocles and Aristotle wrote that the elements weren't just physical but were also spiritual essences. This meant that the elements themselves existed with properties outside the physical, and they could be reached that way. Plato wrote that the elements could change into each other, which helped scholars to look at the relationships between them.

This magic eventually became used in medicine, to draw out illnesses with stones or plants of the same color as the illness, or to give the patient more of the fiery energy they were lacking by eating a plant that was colored red or tasted hot.

It wasn't as unscientific as that sounds. Indeed, a lot of science itself came from what was called "natural magic"—observation of the relationships between physical objects in nature and what they did to patients or other materials when they interacted. (This was the twin of "ceremonial magic," which involved contacting spirits or angels who weren't of the physical world at all in order to gain knowledge or gifts).

One main figure who advanced the use of correspondences was Paracelsus in the early 1500s. He was a genius at chemistry (who named zinc, among other achievements), but like many scientists from the 1300s onward he also followed ideas of Hermeticism. Working on the Hermetic principle that there is a relationship between what happens in the self and what happens outside in the natural world, he developed the "Doctrine of Signatures," which suggests that the shape or attributes of healing herbs correspond to the effect they could have on humans.

Paracelsus looked at herbs, metals, and shapes, but also the influence of the planets on each of them and on us—but not all of these are necessary when we deal directly with the elements themselves. The elements aren't like many of the items in a list that he would have made; they are purer and have an essential essence that stays the same when many other things in the world change. When we use them for divination, we are going right to the largest forces and most fundamental essences in nature.

Some of the items that feature in today's lists of magical correspondences are therefore provable things that we know from science, such as the Moon's effect on the tides. Others are included because they have been linked to specific gods or emotions from ancient times onward. When we roll dice or cast oracles using these lists, we are tapping into a very old system of linked ideas in Western magic. That system has great power, but it is also extremely good at covering all the situations about which humans ask for advice: life, love, work, success, despair, and challenges. These underlying connections are used in much of Western magic and divination, including contributing to the meanings of the elements in tarot cards.

2

# But Which Associations Does Each Element Have?

CORRESPONDENCES ARE PROPERTIES that each element embodies, from the quiet endurance of Earth to the hot urgency of Fire. This next section gives a quick look at these elements so the reader can develop an instinct for the types of energy in play during any reading. After this we will look at how to cast the oracle and use our knowledge of these properties.

## Air

The main correspondence for the element of Air is intelligence. This pairing has existed since the fifth century BCE (initially by Diogenes of Apollonia) and has been continued by many schools and cultures since.

Voice and sound are possible only because of the vibration of the air around us, so Air is also associated with communication and the delivery of information, including speech and writing.

Unlike dense rock or murky water, Air lets us see clearly for great distances and gives our minds the freedom to quickly fly to new places. This clarity helps us use logic and discernment: the ability to make rational decisions unclouded by the emotions that other elements bring.

As well as carrying sounds, the breezes bring smells to us. This adds another mental skill to the list of correspondences because smell is the most effective way to recall memories. Air soon became linked to all purely mental capabilities.

A critical point about the approach of Air is that it is less emotional than Water or Fire. It is detached from the worldly pleasures and physical needs of Earth, and Air can concentrate on precise answers without distraction. There is also a very physical connection, since we must breathe air into our lungs constantly and use it to power our muscles, but despite this it can remain "flighty" and difficult to catch, whipping invisibly one way and then the other. It is a very fast element, with little weight.

The potentially negative aspects of Air are also mostly to do with the mind: when a person is removed from worldly concerns, they can lose sight of reality and retreat into their thoughts. Faster thoughts can lead to anxiety and paranoia, or rigid thinking, which follows rules in a book but ignores emotional needs.

Air can be peaceful and fair, unaffected by hot emotion, but it can also be stunningly effective when used aggressively—fast, focused, and with nothing to hold it back.

The color most associated with Air in magical correspondences is yellow, due to its link to intellect. (This doesn't always feel like a natural color for the Air that we experience!) Others include sky-blue, white and gray, or clear. Shapes include birds, feathers, and symbols depicting the wind, and weapons include swords and daggers.

Air is assigned to the number 1 on the dice, because it can be seen as a lone point high above the land. It can be lonely, unaffected by others, and the solitude of the high mountain peak does not require a partner or distraction.

## Fire

The correspondences of Fire are those we feel when having Fire in our mind or heart: passion, willpower and determination, courage, and drive. Fire is an element of very high energy, giving motivation and power. It is excitable and fast-moving.

It is also transformative, aggressively breaking down material, ending life, and creating the opportunity for new growth afterward. It's easy to see the negative effects: physical destruction and violent emotions that too easily turn to anger, vengeance, or acting without thinking. It powers a lot of our primal drives such as hunger, lust and attraction, and hate for those who threaten us.

While this is a chaotic and potentially dangerous element, the high energy and power can lead to incredibly effective change if harnessed safely. Fire can also be entirely beneficial, providing heat and illumination in the cold night for cooking food and boiling water to keep us alive.

Fire is not difficult to understand. There is little mystery or deception, but lots of raw power. When it appears in a reading, change is going to happen (or if Fire is the current element and a new, calmer one is replacing it, then things will inevitably slow down). Fire is linked to willpower and courage, so making the change happen might be easier than you think when it lends power to your muscles and mind. It is exciting, and noisy. It doesn't stop to ask permission.

In particular, it's worth keeping in mind the amount of sexual attraction covered by Fire. Gentle admiration and mild caring don't belong here as they are not strong enough to lead to physical passion or lust. Loving emotions at a strong level, where the want for this person or determination to protect them is a burning need in the heart, characterize this element. Anything that would inspire you to urgent, passionate action belongs at least partly here and not elsewhere.

The main color associated with Fire is the obvious one: red, but orange and yellow are also linked. Symbols include every type of flame shape, red gems, and magical wands or staves.

Fire is assigned to the number 2 on the die because it often needs a partner. Whether this is fuel it must consume, a target for hot emotions, a goal it is powering toward or something that its light is revealing, Fire frequently engages in a dance around another.

## Water

Water correspondences include some of the most compassionate but also most deadly actions. It is strongly linked to life, healing, and purification, to the gentler and more loving emotions we can experience, and to dreams and prophecy.

Water is mysterious and changeable. It can be a calm lake or a raging sea. It can bestow feelings of peacefulness but also turmoil and heavy grief. This volatility runs through everything it does—how it moves and also how we regularly encounter it in multiple forms. We know it as liquid water, vapor and steam, snow and ice.

This element is especially linked to love and all the sweetness and sadness that comes with it. Instead of Fire's hot lust, Water mingles with everything and brings compassion and empathy.

Our bodies physically contain a lot of water and we can see it present in our blood. Pure, clean water is essential for life, and saltwater from the sea is strong at drawing out infection.

But Water has also played a far less beneficial role in folklore. While it can take away our hurts and bury pains and offerings down into the deep, there is also a side that is deadly and untrustworthy. It has a reputation for lies and deception, fear, illusions, and the kind of emotions that lead to spite and jealousy. For every healing goddess of love connected to the sea there are Sirens and monsters who will deceive and kill.

Where Air is clear over long distances, Water is murky and changeable. It can contain great prizes, including caring, healing, joy, and love, but it also holds unknown and fearsome things, untrustworthy illusions, and sorrow. When Water appears in readings its meaning depends heavily on the position: it is not a strong foundation for Earth to sit upon, and it has no fuel for Fire to use.

Water's color is traditionally blue or blue-green. Its shapes are those of waves and water drops. Symbols include cups and chalices of all kinds.

Water is number 3 on the die because it is more complex than a binary answer. It is not as ordered or solid as the square four, but rides a rising or falling diagonal line.

# Earth

The set of correspondences assigned to Earth have three main themes. The first is from the image of rock: hard, enduring, strong—a mighty and patient defense. The second is from the fertile soil, which gives life and restores natural balance. This is softer and full of green potential. And the third is in how this element relates to human concerns, where it represents material things such as money, work, and all physical needs of the body: hearty food, home comforts and security, and matters of family.

It is the mountain's silent endurance and weight that characterizes Earth in many divination systems. Dependable and tough, this reassures the emotions and slows the pace of life.

In this oracle it also takes on meanings based on the position over or under another element. Unlike Earth's traditional dependability, a great amount of rock suspended over empty Air is not a stable situation.

There are many negatives that can be linked to the properties of Earth. So much weight and stillness can lead to inertia and laziness. The focus on work and home can cause a person who should be pursuing spiritual goals to be greedy for material wealth or personal gain instead.

Being the opposite of Air's free, weightless leaping between new ideas, Earth simply isn't very imaginative. It can promote tolerance of others by providing security for the self but may reject new proposals if they are presented too quickly. It clings to tradition even when that tradition is authoritarian or oppressive.

Generally, however, Earth is a reassuring and positive force. It includes the environment healthy for life, provides walls against fears and success in wealth. We experience it within our bodies as the structure and toughness of our bones.

Earth's color is usually brown, green, or black. Its shapes include mountains and stones, but also wood, trees, and animals if concentrating on its life-giving aspects. Its symbols are often pentacles and coins.

The number assigned to Earth on the die is 4, a neatly ordered, symmetrical, solid square of dots.

## Sun

The brightest light in the sky brings all kinds of beneficial and powerful blessings. It gives warmth, health, and light—the energy needed for life. It dismisses the darkness to show what was previously hidden and brings the truth into the light where it can be seen. This revelation has caused it to be linked to science, knowledge, and law.

Most of all it confers success. In any endeavor, in any situation, the Sun is primarily a sign of great success and happiness.

Although its character can change a little at dawn and sunset, it is seen as much more constant than the Moon's many phases.

It is also a friend to mankind, growing crops, giving light, and keeping bodies healthy.

The Sun has a particularly complex relationship to Fire. It is stronger than every form of fire naturally encountered on Earth, so readings such as "The Guildmaster" (where the Sun is weaker than the existing amount of Fire in the situation) need more attention than usual. A weak Sun is still vastly more powerful than a bonfire, and the meaning is usually that of a skillful master choosing to hold back their might. The Sun is so powerful and so linked with success, even a small amount of it in a reading can still affect the entire meaning.

The other Fire and Sun combinations also carry an aspect of this, always aware that one is a student and the other a master.

When in combination with other elements, the Sun behaves in similar ways to Fire: high energy, strong and righteous motivation, but with less danger of chaotic upset. In fact, good outcomes are strongly likely, along with luck, health, and success.

The negative aspects of Sun are in its great power. Drought and deserts come from its heat, and when all shadows are dismissed by its unrelenting gaze there is little room for mystery in life. Science is a great gift for the world, but it can be unforgiving if not used with compassion. The same is true of religion, where strict authoritarian laws lead to imbalance. Unlike the Moon's shelter for taboo activities in semidarkness, the Sun has traditional associations with patriarchal law and the orderly restrictions of society.

Sun's colors are yellow or gold, and its shape is a circle with the dot in the center, or a circle with rays around the edge.

The number assigned to the Sun on the die is 5. It is a high energy, exciting number, with dots radiating around a central point.

## Moon

In a similar way to the Sun being linked with Fire, many of the Moon's properties have a crossover with Water. The Moon governs dreams and reaches to our deeper emotions. It is the opposite of the Sun's fixed light, instead being an ever-changing rise and fade of reflection that gives moonlight, shadows, and sometimes sheltering darkness to those in the night below.

The Moon is linked to magic and mystery, the unknown, intuition, and hidden knowledge. It travels at night and changes the phase that we can see. It pulls at the waters and was believed to conjure up wild emotions. It certainly inspires our imaginations like no other sight: when it shines a full light onto the land below, that illumination is a beautiful silver and white.

The magical and philosophical correspondences of the Moon concentrate on its mystical aspects. The more powerful the influence of the Moon on us, the more unworldly or disconnected from mundane reality we feel. A reading with only Moon energy in it would have no connection to the grounding energy of Earth or reassuring known truth of the Sun. In the oracle it frequently symbolizes the arrival of magic, as well as bringing remote beauty and an escape from the normal world.

The colors associated with the Moon are silver and white, and sometimes black and white if depicting the phases. Its shape is usually represented as a crescent or full circle.

The number assigned to the moon on the die is 6, the maximum it is possible to gain, set out in two full and balanced rows, which signify a complete inner understanding.

# How to Cast the Oracle

EACH READING TAKES the form of a new influence coming into an existing situation.

This is shown by having two elements, one "over" the other. The top one is the new arrival, either weaker or stronger than the existing element below it, which is of medium strength:

**New Element 1**
**Over**
**Existing Element 2**

This leads to readings such as "Lesser Air over Fire."

Each of these combinations has also been given a title and an image. Lesser Air over Fire is "The Bellows." During the divination you will roll three dice (or one die, three times).

The first number determines the top element (element 1).

The second number is the bottom element (element 2), and the third gives the strength of element 1: either greater or lesser than the medium-strength element 2.

If rolling three dice, you can arrange them as follows: place the die for element 1, then place element 2 underneath it, then add the third die to the right of the element 1 (showing its greater or lesser strength).

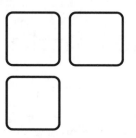

| Dice 1 | Dice 2 | Dice 3 |
|--------|--------|--------|
| 1: Air | 1: Air | 1–3: Lesser |
| 2: Fire | 2: Fire | |
| 3: Water | 3: Water | |
| 4: Earth | 4: Earth | 4–6: Greater |
| 5: Sun | 5: Sun | |
| 6: Moon | 6: Moon | |

An example would therefore be: 3, 4, 1.

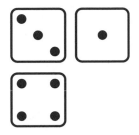

Remember that the dice are: "new element 1 over existing element 2, then strength of element 1."

This is therefore "Lesser Water over Earth," titled "The Rains." You can then go to the page for that entry, and read the meaning given.

There is much more that you can do while casting the oracle. You can prepare the dice themselves for divination work with a consecration ritual, and prepare yourself as well—clearing your mind of the influences from your day and feeling the presence of the elements more strongly. Rituals and meditations for doing this are included in a later section.

# How to Ask the Questions

YOU CAN ASK any type of question of this oracle. You do not need to phrase it for a yes or no answer, and you can ask about all points of the future or past.

The oracle's readings describe a change in energy because of the relationship between two elements. Each answer contains a lot of information, meaning that instead of just "Yes," it will say "Yes—in this way." Or: "Tomorrow will bring this kind of situation." Or: "If you really want that thing to happen, here is what you should do to achieve it and this is what could block it."

Since magical correspondences frequently deal with love, intelligence, anger, patience, success, and other worldly concerns, the answer will often be linked to emotions or attitudes we should adopt or avoid.

It can be helpful to cast the oracle more than once. Tarot cards for example are often drawn in threes, to ask about the past, present, and then the future in one reading. This oracle can be used in the same way or in the formats listed below.

**One reading (rolling 3 dice):** A new influence, which will come between now and tomorrow.

**Two readings:** The first shows more detail on the present situation, and the second reading is the near future.

**Three readings:** The first is the present, and the next two are choices that you can make for the future. Look carefully at the benefits and dangers of each. They are both possibilities that you can take if you steer events using the tools or attitude given in the answer.

**Many readings over time:** If there is a question that is long-term, or that you wish to ask more than once, it can be useful to keep a journal and ask it over a period of time. This can show us how we change, but also whether we have been ignoring earlier good advice!

**Two readings—how should I do this?** The oracle can be excellent at telling you the best approach to take to achieve your goal. In this case both the readings are set in the near future, but one gives a strategy for success and the other is a danger to be avoided.

If you have a particular element that you wish to take to represent yourself, to influence the reading or as a starting point (similar to using a querent card in tarot), then there are steps you can take to align your mind with the element before casting the oracle. You can wear clothing or items symbolizing one of them, with the colors or shapes given in the previous section on correspondences. In the later section "Magic and Rituals," there are meditations and other ideas on how to connect more deeply to one or all of the elements. For now we'll go on to see some example readings that were cast during the writing of this book.

# Three Example Readings

## Example 1

A friend asked me to read the oracle for her regarding work. She was stuck in her current job and planned to apply for a new one, but it was risky and would involve moving house if it all went ahead.

I cast the oracle twice, once to clarify the current situation and a second to show the best path to take in the near future.

The first reading was 4-4-6—Greater Earth over Earth, called "The Mountain."

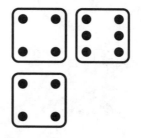

With so much solid Earth energy it's an incredibly safe combination, but there is no movement at all to anywhere new. If you don't like the current situation, then this could be very frustrating. It said that she would be safe where she is, and her career would not suffer, but it was also not surprising if she felt that nothing would change there.

The future reading was 5-2-4—Greater Sun over Fire, "The Knighthood."

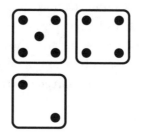

This shows Fire being the current situation and the Sun coming in to replace it. This is a nice answer, with the Sun being so strongly linked to success.

However, to get there, it has to start with the high energy, risk, and change that Fire brings. This very clearly said that my friend had a choice: she could stay exactly where she was, as the unmoving mountain, or take the risk and be rewarded with the Sun's great success.

## Example 2

Of course I'm regularly asked for divinations about love. A woman wasn't sure whether to become more serious with her partner, or even exactly how to do that.

The oracle gave 6-3-2—Lesser Moon over Water, "The Still Soul."

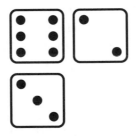

This was actually surprising. I was expecting something with Fire, passion, attraction, or Water's bonds of love coming in strongly. From the way that she'd described the relationship, I thought it needed more Fire to warm things up and make fun changes. Instead, while Water is definitely the subject (not unusual when the question is about love) and the Lesser Moon only a small influence beside it, this reading doesn't have very much to do with two people at all. It is about looking inside for answers in calm and meaningful silence: the waters of our deep emotions lit subtly by the beautiful glow of the Moon, connecting us to mysteries and inner knowledge. This reading says, "You might already know the answer, but you need to get away from all the background noise to see it." I'd been expecting to give some examples of loud, fun things to do to revitalize a relationship, but this said just the opposite, that she needed stillness and quiet to see her feelings clearly and make good decisions.

## Example 3

Another friend asked for an oracle about happiness. He just couldn't settle his mind that week, felt uncomfortable and disconnected. He wanted to do some magical work to break out of it and was asking which direction would be most effective.

I cast an oracle with just one reading. It gave 2-4-1—Lesser Fire over Earth, "Tending the Campfire."

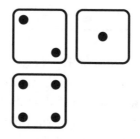

Again, this was a surprise. The oracle gives a very wide range of answers on types of magic, or approaches to problems. It has many that involve a lot of excitement. It could have said that he should get out of the house and do new things or concentrate on feeling strong and positive Sun energy. It could have given many types of answers involving the magic of the Moon, or Air's intellect in writing or accomplishing clever new things. Instead it said: take care of the basics. Eat, sleep, and keep your house running comfortably. Take time to look after yourself and rest. (He then admitted that he'd been working and socializing so much during that week that sleep hadn't really happened!)

6

# Choosing Your Dice

IT CAN BE easy to find or buy one six-sided die, but you should
also consider collecting a number of dice to use. There are many
types available, such as wooden, metal, and patterned. You could
choose to look for a matching set or deliberately have three dice
of different colors so that you can assign them to be element 1,
element 2, or the greater–lesser dice.

Dice can be beautiful objects, or just usefully small items that
can be carried in a pocket. You can begin rolling them immediately
and consulting the pages in this book for answers, or you can take
an approach with more ritual in it. Divination is a way for us to call
on the elemental powers of nature and to follow centuries of tradition by performing a magical action to look into the mysteries of

the future. If you wish to make your dice into magical tools, a later section will show how you can consecrate them with all of the elements, as well as how to prepare yourself to make a reading.

# Advanced Ways to Read the Oracle

WE'VE SEEN HOW the three dice lead to an entry with just one title, but there are still several ways that we can interpret each combination after that point.

You can simply read the definition given in the entry. This is always the main one, and the whole oracle can be read using only this method. It will give information about the correspondences involved and the usual ways in which these interact.

Once you feel you know the elements well, you may find that you can go to just the names of the two elements and create your own meaning instead of reading the pages here. This is the method that will rely on the most intuition from the reader, and it is valid. The basic part of the reading here is "one element over another," and the interpretations after that point can be less fixed. The detailed descriptions on each page build on the pairing, but if you see different things in the interplay of energies than is written here, you should pursue those meanings as well. This is an especially good route if you have your own knowledge of the tarot or elemental correspondences, such as those given earlier in this book.

Intuition is not everyone's favorite path, and there is one further method you can use that can answer some of the deeper questions more precisely, using a total of five dice instead of three.

Here is an example of this more precise approach. If the reading is 3-2-5 (Greater Water over Fire), then it suggests that the Water has come into the situation and successfully replaced or overcome the existing Fire. However, there are two main things we don't yet know that could change how you react to this:

- Is this reading telling you that the best outcome will be found if you are the Water and you choose to put out the Fire?

- Or is the Water another person who you should be wary of and your Fire being extinguished something that you should fight against?

Now that we've learnt about the correspondences associated with each element, we know that Fire could represent your own passion and determination being smothered by lots of unwanted, negative watery emotion. The reading could therefore be a warning.

It is fine to use just the 3 dice as already described and leave the remaining details entirely up to your intuition. This was always a primary way of using this oracle. However, if you would like the reading to be more specific, you can roll another two dice:

## Dice 4
**1–3.** The new element (as depicted by dice 1) is **you.**
**4–6.** The new element (as depicted by dice 1) is **someone else.**

## Dice 5
**1–3.** This is a good outcome for you.
**4–6.** This is a warning against this outcome.

Going back to our original reading of 3-2-5, we can add these extra dice for more information: 3-2-5-6-2.

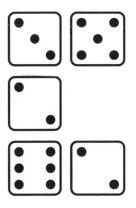

*Greater Water over Fire,*
*Someone Else, Good Outcome*

Now the Water putting out the Fire is definitely someone else affecting the situation, not you. However, the Fire being put out is actually a good result for you, so this person is helping. Maybe you are too angry and need someone to stop you going too far, or maybe the Water is the forceful introduction of loving emotions into a wider general situation of conflict.

While this level of detail can be confusing if you haven't read the pages for the combinations yet, there is one more aspect of advanced reading to discuss.

"Greater" elements, where a stronger force comes into the situation, usually succeed at changing the medium-strength current situation. "Lesser" elements try to make a change but fail.

They do not always fail though. Sometimes a reading of "Lesser" can be someone using deliberately gentle and supportive emotions to dampen your fire to a steadier level, but not put it out. They could choose the restrained level of strength and still achieve their goal, instead of the more typical definition (which is that Lesser fails because it doesn't have enough Water to entirely replace the Fire).

This is a highly intuitive oracle, and even with all five dice there can still be room for interpretation. Try making some readings with just three first, and then later with five. Once you have seen the play of elements meeting each other with their correspondences a few times, it should be easier to settle on just one answer each time.

Don't be worried by this complexity! You do not have to use any of the techniques in this advanced section: the oracle can be simply the dice and the definitions on the page. If you wish to take it further once you are familiar with it, then come back here and try some of these routes.

8

# Beyond Dice

IT IS ALSO possible to use other systems to arrive at these readings, not just dice. You could, for example, paint the image given with each combination onto a card and perform a divination using only the deck of cards. (This would give you seventy-two images.) If the art is too difficult, you could simply write the title of each combination (such as "The Tranquil Lake") and the two elements involved onto the card (with Greater/Lesser for the first one).

This is totally valid and will not change the probabilities of any answer appearing. I recommend dice because they are easily bought and carried, have a long history of being used in oracles, and have given excellent results over several years. However, any system that arrives at "Greater or Lesser Element 1 over Element 2" with an equal probability of any result appearing will generate this oracle.

If you do want to develop your own deck from the images suggested, or from any that come to you when you work with the combinations of elements, then there are many more options for doing so. The cards could be painted as suggested above or printed with photographs or illustrations from the Internet. You could even make a collage with the colors of materials linked to the element involved or laminate the cards to keep the art protected.

Whichever you decide, you can consecrate the cards as described in the next section since they are magical tools you will work with.

Experiment with any new ways that appeal to you, but keep in mind that you shouldn't change the structure in a way that would alter the probability of any readings appearing. The oracle can only give out what you allow to be there in the first place, and the elements should all be given equal chance.

9

# Magic and Rituals for Using the Oracle

THIS SECTION GIVES optional rituals and magical workings that can bring more depth to your interactions with the elements. You do not have to use any of these, but they can be invaluable for readers who wish to add more to their practice.

The first two are a ritual for consecrating your dice as magical tools and a ritual to use while performing readings. After this there are meditations on each of the elements that can bring you closer to understanding the pure elements themselves.

# A Ritual for Consecrating the Dice

The dice that you use for divination are magical tools, much like tarot cards. They can be prepared with this special purpose in mind and then only used for divination.

The ritual to consecrate your dice requires several items to help bring the pure elements into the space that you are using. You will need a source for each of the six elements in the oracle—in some cases this is easy, but others may take more effort to arrange. These items can also be used when preparing yourself to read the oracle each time, so they are useful to collect even if you don't wish to consecrate the dice.

Fire is provided very well by a candle of any shape. This can be a typically narrow and tall candle, a thick pillar candle, or even a small tea-light. It should not be scented. Remember that if you are creating fire (even with safety matches) you must always have a means of putting the fire out as well! Keep a candle snuffer and an amount of water nearby in case of accidents.

Air is also easy to arrange for: the best way to provide Air's presence in ritual is as smell. This can be from incense, essential oils, or a scented candle. Taking Air into our lungs along with the information and memories that smell provides to us is a very powerful way to interact with physical Air, and also its magical correspondences.

Water should be present as a bowl, dish, or other container of clean water. This can be bought, come from a household tap, or even collected from rain. River water is often unsafe to collect or drink, so do not think that you have to go to nature for this. Any water will bring the physical wetness, vapor, and moving surface that is needed to represent this element; it does not have to be especially pure. It is a link to the purer ideal essence of the element.

Earth can be represented in a number of ways. A pentacle made of wood is often used for this, providing a solid, grounding base on which to place other items. Wooden plates can also be suitable, given their connections to wood, food, and the home. Alternatively, any heavy stone or rock can work very well as an item to bring the qualities of solidity, strength, and permanence into your space.

The Sun and Moon are obviously more difficult to choose items for! We can't have either of them physically present, so we must find something that represents them in our own minds. This can be any object with a symbol or image of them on it, or colored with gold (Sun) or silver (Moon). It can be art showing each, or crystals colored white or gold.

There is an advanced option, which is to capture the light from the Sun and Moon instead of having an item with their shape: to do this, you should take an item outside when the Sun or Moon can be seen so that their light touches it.

There are several options for the object to use for the Sun: some water, a candle, any yellow crystal, or any gold object.

If you want to use water, then look at the glint of sunlight on its surface. Let the warm energy of the Sun seep into the liquid.

If you want to capture the Sun's light with a candle instead, take a candle outside in sunlight and light it (again, be careful that you can also put the fire out at any time). Let the Sun's burning heat fall onto the candle. You can then put the flame out—when you light it again in ritual, it will act as a smaller fire on a candle that has already seen the Sun. (This must be a separate candle to any of the others used for Fire or the scented candle for Air.)

And if it is a crystal or object, let the sunlight fall onto it.

If you would like to say some words, then an optional announcement is:

"I show this (water/candle/object) the light of the Sun. May it bring the Sun's glorious energy to my oracle work."

The object for the Moon can be a small container of water (it should be separate from the container for the Sun), a mirror, or any object with a shape or color to represent the Moon. A mirror works particularly well, since the Moon's light is itself reflected, and white or clear crystals can also be appropriate.

As you hold this object up for the moonlight to touch, you can say the following line (this is optional; you don't need to say anything but can use this if you wish):

"I show this (water/mirror/object) the light of the Moon. May it bring the Moon's luminous presence to my oracle work."

You only need to choose one of these objects for the Sun, and one for the Moon.

Once you have gathered all six items, you can start the ritual to bring the nature of the elements into your dice. You can keep the book with you for this part and read from it when there are any words to say.

First find a quiet space where you won't be disturbed, and make sure that the surface you are working on is large enough and stable enough to hold candles. Place all the items that you have gathered to represent the elements in that space, as well as your dice.

Begin the ritual by walking around your area in a clockwise circle, and say,

"I prepare this space for the work I am about to do. May it contain the magic and purify the tools I consecrate here today."

Then go to where the items are gathered and light any candles, incense or other items which require fire. Pick up the dice in your hand and hold them near the Air source. Waft the smell from your Air source toward your nose, breathing it in. Then waft it over the dice in your hand, and say,

"I consecrate these tools with the element of Air."

Next go to the candle flame and hold your hand high above it. Slowly find a distance where you can gently feel the heat from the candle on your hand (but not too hot), and say,

"I consecrate these tools with the element of Fire."

(You do not need to have Fire touch your dice directly—its heat and light in the circle are enough.)

Go to the source of water and hold your dice in one hand, dipping the fingers of your other hand into the water. Flick drops of water onto the dice, and say,

"I consecrate these tools with the element of Water."

Next go to the item that represents Earth. Touch each dice to it in turn so that they are in direct contact with its surface, and say,

"I consecrate these tools with the element of Earth."

Move to your Sun item. If it is water, flick drops of the water onto the dice as in the previous Water step. If it is a candle, feel its heat as in the Fire step. If it is an object or image, touch the dice to it as in the Earth step, and say,

"I consecrate these tools with the touch of the Sun."

Finally, use the Moon item. If it is water, flick the water onto the dice as in the Water step. If it is a mirror, hold the dice in front of it so that the light can reach them. If it is another object or image, touch the dice to it as in the Earth step, and say,

"I consecrate these tools with the touch of the Moon."

When all six elements have been used, say,

"These tools are now purified and consecrated by the elements."

The ritual is then complete. Put the dice down and walk the circle around your space counterclockwise, to release the magical energies and return the space to the mundane world. As you do this, say

"I take down my circle and release its energies, my work within it is done."

## A Ritual for Casting the Oracle

The oracle can be read without using a ritual, but magical preparation is always useful. It helps to clear our head of the events of the day, and to remember all the details of the tools and forces we are about to work with.

You will need an object representing each of the elements for this ritual. The previous consecration ritual also required these, so you can use the objects from there if you have gathered them. Otherwise look back at that section for the description of six suitable items.

Before you begin, make sure that you have a large flat surface onto which you can roll the dice. You should also put the six elemental items in front of you, somewhere they can be reached easily but where they will not stop the rolling of the dice.

Clear your mind and take some slow, deep breaths. Concentrate on the question you are planning to ask and how many readings you intend to perform. You do not need to have a specific question in mind: the oracle can talk about the present day and how it will change in the near future without being prompted with specific questions. Alternatively you can ask it a question before rolling, and apply the answer to that.

The first step is to bring the elements to yourself. We will go in the order of the numbers on the dice, so the first element is Air. Take the incense, scented candle or other source of scent and breathe it in. Feel the message carried on the air enter your body and feel your brain unlock the secrets it contains.

Hold your hands above the candle flame representing Fire. (Not too close, and don't touch it directly!) Feel the heat and look into the light.

Dip your fingers into the container of Water. Feel its wetness, coolness—see how its shape moves and flows.

Touch the object representing Earth. Feel its solidity and stillness, similar to the vast Earth beneath you.

Turn to the Sun object that has been in sunlight (this is typically water, a crystal or other object shaped or colored to link to the Sun, or a candle). Picture the light and heat of the Sun in your mind. Feel its life-giving rays, its burning success. Let its warmth gently dissolve any obstacles in your way.

Turn to the Moon object. Picture the pure, white energy of the Moon filling your mind and body. Feel its peaceful and mysterious light.

Now pick up the dice and form your question or questions. Roll the dice when you are ready, and consult the book.

# Meditations for Connecting Yourself More Deeply to the Elements

It can be useful to devote time to each of the elements in turn, to experience them more fully. This will help with your understanding of their energies and your connection to them.

The next pages give six meditations that can be performed to help you explore the elements. As with all the rituals in this book, they are totally optional, but they can bring more experience to your reading of the oracle and elemental divination in general.

## Air Meditation

Sit comfortably and close your eyes. Take a deep breath, feeling the Air entering your lungs. Let it out slowly, and take another.

Breathe in through your nose and out through your mouth. Feel your chest rise and fall as you do this.

Now open your eyes and concentrate on smell. Focus on all the things that you can smell in the area. Move to a place nearby that has a different smell (around the room if you are indoors, or to trees or flowers if you are outside). Experience the smell coming in from outside your body, into your nose, and being recognized by your brain. Continue to take slow, calm breaths.

Sit down again and close your eyes. Listen to the sounds brought to you by the vibration of air. Feel the world around you, communicating through Air.

With your eyes closed, picture a vast open sky, with yourself as a bird flying in it. There is only empty space and supporting winds in any direction. You can see to the horizon, and far below to the ground, but that is too remote to worry about. Feel your daily concerns fade away along with the emotions that push you. At this height, nothing blocks your thoughts from moving forward as far and fast as you wish. If you think of an idea, or recall a memory, it can be seen in your mind clearly and without any other emotional baggage. You are alone here, free to journey in the direction that you want and able to see clearly all around you.

The sky is supportive, quiet, and calming. Take deep breaths of the pure air and explore what it feels like not to be surrounded by walls.

When you are ready, open your eyes and readjust to your normal mental pace.

### Fire Meditation

Find an area indoors where you will not be disturbed and can light a candle safely. Arrange to have a candle, matches, or other means of lighting it, and a way to put out any fire if it is accidentally knocked over (this is just a precaution you should always take).

Light the candle and look at the flame. Cup your hands near to it so that you can feel the heat.

That heat is also in your blood. There is electricity and energy shooting around your body all the time. Food is broken down in your belly, used as fuel to power movement just as wood is consumed in a bonfire to make heat and light.

Study the candle flame and imagine your whole body made of the same fire, but more powerful. Your arms and legs become full of intense heat and barely-contained power, and you want to run just to burn up the overwhelming energy. Your mind becomes wild—passionate, determined, needing to race and jump and live.

Fire is the element of force, speed, and aggression, but it also contains beauty and joy. It is active and leaps to make change happen. Spend a few moments thinking about the actions you would take if you felt no fear, only a firm conviction to act on the things that give you joy. Think about how you would move—quickly forward, directly to your goal, fearless and determined. Feel your whole being light up hot and clean, purified with fire all the way through, ready to act quickly when you gather your willpower to throw toward a new challenge.

Put out the candle, but remember the feeling of energy and power that came from the Fire.

## Water Meditation

If you have access to a bath, then that is one of the most effective ways to explore the element of water safely. (If you do not, then there is another route given below.) Feel the water surrounding your body and limbs, and make it move gently. Feel the back and forth flowing of the wave, on the surface and below. The water outside your body is continued in your blood, matching the liquid beneath your skin to the element you are surrounded by. Feel your blood, rushing and moving around your head, arms, chest, legs, like a river that turns back on itself continually. Feel the internal waves circulating through you.

If a bath isn't suitable, then take a glass of water. Sit down somewhere quiet where you will not be disturbed, and set the glass in front of you. Drink the water, taking it into your body. Feel it go down your throat and be sent to refresh and heal all the parts you need it to. New blood can be produced—digestion and the creation of energy can be supported.

Most of our body is water, but we don't think of it that way. The simple liquid is crucial for life—we die in days without it. It also teaches us a way to be, to move, to adapt.

Water parts quickly and changes course instantly. If something blocks its way, water flows around it. We can do this as well, although sometimes we forget that it is an option! Picture yourself on a busy street in a crowd of people. You can ignore what they do and just walk in a completely straight line, bumping into many, clashing with force and straining your muscles. Alternatively, you can choose to be only slightly slower and flow into all the gaps that are created near you. If someone approaches, give way. If an opportunity arises, take it. Your progress forward is not as important as keeping a relaxed mind.

Holding on to this calm feeling instead of being led by mental anxiety or forceful physical demands is a good way to experience the wisdom of water.

### Earth Meditation
Find a place outdoors or indoors where you will not be disturbed, and sit down.

Close your eyes and feel the solid Earth beneath you. If you can put your hands on the ground or the floor, do so.

Feel the structure of everything beneath you supporting your weight, ultimately resting on miles of dense rock. Extend this feeling downward, anchoring yourself to the Earth.

Feel this anchor through the soles of your feet, or more parts of your body if you are able to sit directly on the floor or ground. Even if you are in a room of a house, feel the tough, unbending materials doing the job of holding you up and not giving in, rock's enduring stillness not wavering.

In our bodies the Earth is our bones, the hard structure that carries the rest. Feel those bones in your limbs and in the ribs inside your chest. Imagine the rest of your body as tough as the rock beneath you, as if your chest is surrounded by a shell of heavy stone that protects you and doesn't crack. Emotions and doubts have no place in that shield's character for stone simply goes on without fear. It doesn't change its mind quickly or become bored—it has patience. We can have those aspects too when we set ourselves to be as resilient as rock.

When we think of the element of Earth, we also think of the green life upon it. Without the life in the ground, our own life wouldn't be possible: Earth's second character in correspondences is that of the fertile soil. It is healthy, giving nourishment and stability to slow-growing plants.

As well as taking in the lessons of patience and endurance, we should feel thankful to Earth for the renewing and dependable life force of our own growth and that of the natural world.

## Sun Meditation

If possible, do this meditation where you can see direct sunlight, either indoors or outdoors.

Sit quietly and take a slow breath. Feel the Sun shining down from above, providing heat and light to the planet below. This light is purer and stronger than any fires we can see or create for ourselves on the surface.

Draw the yellow-white light down into your body, filling your limbs. Picture a healthy, energy-giving Sun inside your chest, radiating that light from within and powering your movement. Feel it clean and purify you all the way through. It is constant, not flickering, and joyous. As it cleans away the pointless worries that we carry with us from our daily lives, it reveals our true selves. It gently but persistently seeks out every hidden detail beneath its gaze, bringing it to where we can see the truth.

We are connected to the Sun for all aspects of life. Without it we would not be able to grow food, but our bodies also directly use it to create vitamins and stay healthy. It affects our emotions and moods in a huge way. On a physical level we are even more connected: every atom of carbon, calcium, every protein, our blood, our brain … everything physical was created in a Sun out in the universe. They are the engines that create heavier elements when they burn and send those elements out into space when they explode. Every one of us is literally made from stardust, because nothing is made of anything else.

Feel yourself connected to this higher source of power and life. Use its energy for success and its purity to remind you of the ideals that you could work toward.

## Moon Meditation

Perform this meditation at night, on any day of the month.

The Moon hangs as a lonely beauty in the night sky, but unlike the constant Sun, it is always dimming and brightening. It goes through a cycle, changing how much it will let us see of its surface throughout the month. When the Moon is full it is a gentle lamp, but the Moon also hides away and allows darkness to blanket the land.

The Moon has always provoked our dreams and imaginations. When we picture its light and shadow, we are pulled into contemplating mysteries.

Take a deep breath and close your eyes. See the Full Moon in the night sky, slowly changing shape to a crescent and then becoming entirely dark. See it grow again from the other side, back into a full circle.

The Moon is linked to our mind. It stirs our intuition and pulls at us just as it does to the tides. Draw the Full Moon's light down to the center of your forehead. Imagine a white disc there, a Moon fixed and giving its power to your thoughts.

In the calm surroundings of a landscape lit only by its pale radiance, look inside yourself. Go inside, to your real wants and needs, to the person you hide from the world and would be if you could have enough stillness and silence. Steer your way with intuition and magic, in a place away from society's laws and attention, to a private and hidden chamber.

When we cast oracles, we can use this quiet concentration to shut out the noise from the world and hear the answers given in divination.

# The Oracle

THIS SECTION GIVES the primary definition for each combination, a description of an image associated with it, and then possible alternative meanings and extra guidance.

It is important to remember that the reading is not just the title (e.g., "The Tranquil Lake"). The real reading is the combination of elements, for example "Lesser Air over Water," and the final meaning of that is highly dependent on the reader and their life that day.

The elemental oracle gives predictions for the movement of energy and fate, and the context can be provided by your intuition. The following definitions are therefore not all the possible answers—only a typical interpretation that you can modify or ignore if another feels more correct.

Combinations are grouped together in this book by the existing second element—the medium-strength one that is being changed.

This is because it is the one that describes the current situation, and the Greater/Lesser element coming above it is the near future—which can still be altered if you work against it. This section therefore lists the readings as twelve " ... over Air" and then twelve " ... over Fire." You can find the combination you need that way, or by referring to the table at the back of this book, which gives the page number of each and a short summary of their meanings.

This oracle has brought much wisdom and
happiness already, and I hope it gives each of you
the most enriching and inspirational experiences.

# Greater Air over Air

## THE FREE SKIES

Freedom; the chance to soar wildly in uncrowded spaces

...........

*A falcon flying in wind-filled skies*
*with clear sight to the horizon.*

THIS IS A reading filled with potential and flight. It is Air over Air: there are no foundations of rock to hold you down or keep your goals realistic, only an empty sky into which come even stronger winds to lift you up. The falcon in the image has clear sight over great distances and is able to take quick, decisive action.

This strong new wind successfully overpowers the existing status quo of the previous Air with its own plans. Air's connection to speech and communication means that the new influence could be a booming voice dominating the conversation, or an academic paper beating an intellectual challenge. It is often about succeeding at a mental challenge posed by another.

There are many opportunities in this pairing, as it has the most open space in the oracle and no boundaries or constricting traditions that you need to conform to. Greater Air over Air means that there is enough to fill your lungs, enough to soar up and dive down without fear of running out of space. Instead of feeling blocked in, there is endless healthy open sky where your thoughts can fly forward and you can reach important answers without distraction from emotions or physical demands. As long as the wind's currents are ridden with discipline, then this combination signifies an empowering and supportive thrust speeding you toward new answers.

Such freedom can also be a hazard, however. No other element acts as a support here, so you could find yourself thrown about unexpectedly: spinning out of control and unable to find solid ground. For example, with this much mental energy, it is easy to give in to fears that are entirely in your head. You will be able to make great leaps of intellect, but this can take you very quickly into insecurities that aren't based in reality.

Having no Earth present means that you have no foundations that could help keep you upright in the strong winds. However, the absence of Water or Fire does mean that you are not caught up in emotional turmoil while trying to think, which is usually helpful. Air's single dot on the die is alone because devoting time to thought often requires calm concentration. This is the loneliness of the calm hermit high on a mountain, contemplating all that they see in the clouds.

When this combination is seen it usually signifies success at a mental challenge. You might think your way out of a difficult situation, or succeed academically. In each reading, we look at what is present but also what is missing—in this case there is no opposite influence to Air at all, nothing heavy or grounding, nothing that would keep you from getting lost in the clouds. Use all this available space … but check in afterward and make sure that you aren't neglecting issues around the home or family in the excitement of mental flights in a vast open world.

# Lesser Air over Air

## The Advisor

Subtle and wise advice, careful steering,
skillful flying between turbulent currents

...........

*A careful person whispering advice into the ear of a Ruler.*

WHERE THE EXISTING situation is Air (usually concerning matters of thought or communication), one of the positive meanings of Lesser Air is of someone choosing not to dominate but instead to deliberately use a quiet voice. The Lesser Air is like a knife carefully inserted in the calm spaces between wild winds. This combination often signifies wise advice from a sensible source: they let the stronger air blow and choose to act when the time is right. The advice will be of the best sort and you should listen for it instead of ignoring it in favor of the louder voices.

Most lesser influences also carry an aspect of failure, however, as they are not powerful enough to overcome the existing element. In this case it could be someone shouting into the wind but being unheard. Air's correspondences mean that this possible defeat is usually of an intellectual nature, so the initial Air could be a puzzle (which the new influence was not sufficient to overcome). If this occurs, there are two answers: to take an even more intellectual approach in an attempt to bring Greater Air to the problem and succeed, or if you don't feel you have the mental reserves for that, to bring in a different element. A reading with two Air elements in it has no structure at all, no ties to the Earth, not even the strong guiding lights of the Sun or Moon to speak to the inner self. You can look at the actions available to you—at Fire's bold challenge, Water's accepting embrace, the Moon's untamed intuition—and use these to solve the problem instead.

Lesser Air can also mean we feel unable to breathe as the storm whirls around us. The key is to concentrate on being lesser until you are ready: quietly focusing on yourself, getting air into your lungs, gathering your wits. If a problem is too difficult, pull your mental focus inward until you have recovered your balance. The strong winds can blow you upside down, so the first step is to learn to right yourself within them. Then you can look at whether to bring a new approach to the issue instead of trying again with more Air.

Lesser Air is a chance to withdraw and look for allies. You don't have to be alone, and even if the help that a friend acting as the Advisor gives is also Air, this is an opportunity to look around at the wisdom that any of the other elements could bring before proceeding.

# Greater Fire over Air

## PASSION

Soaring joy and determination, the heart overruling the head

...........

*Two people happily kissing and embracing.*

INTELLECTUAL AIR IS met here by a stronger fire, which ignores detached thought in favor of a bright passion! The Fire comes roaring in, replacing the freedom and contemplation of Air with an adrenaline-filled shout for determined adventure.

Both Fire and Water have associations with emotion, but those belonging to Fire are more urgent: courage, lust, anger, and high energy. This can bring fantastic new experiences to a stale situation or warmth and focus where there was previously empty space. It means an increased speed and less time for contemplation or logic: Fire is more interested in chasing down what it wants.

The image for this reading is of two lovers, and in relationships it brings a joyous, carefree energy and momentum. The caution and detached planning of Air are swept aside and the lovers are able to make the decisions that their hearts already pull them toward. Indeed, in any aspect of life (including academic tasks), if you have been holding back before you reveal your passion, the Greater Fire here says that now is the time to start moving.

This new rush dominating all thought can of course lead to a lack of wisdom. Impatient action ruled by high energy has a danger of being foolish, so if a force this disruptive is entering into play, be careful to use it properly! Fire is an amazing resource—it motivates us, drives us forward, gives us all the energy we need to overcome obstacles, and burns brightly. But it also does the things that we try to stop in our daily lives, such as escaping our control and burning us, our houses, or anything that acts as fuel.

Although there is a need for caution, this is also one of the happiest readings. It shows a love or eagerness for action that can cause our heart to leap and our bodies to feel full of life and determination. Run with it, ride it, seize it … but do check in afterward that you didn't let the fire get out of control. Rejoice that mental plans have become movement but (as with most times that Greater Fire is found in this oracle) also take a moment to ensure that you aren't going outside safe boundaries.

# Lesser Fire over Air

## THE SNUFFED CANDLE

Hasty passions are rejected by clear thought;
it is not yet time to put plans into action

...........

*A candle, just blown out by a strong wind,*
*with smoke still curling up from its wick.*

THE OBVIOUS READING for this combination is that the Fire fails to replace Air and instead has its energy rejected by the less emotional, calmer Air. This can be positive: Fire's potentially explosive emotion is now guided by rational thinking and directed with greater precision.

Fire and Air together can erupt, but in this case that danger is defeated by rational plans or unclouded thought. Aggression is rejected. Any exuberant actions will be controlled by the more powerful mental restraint that Air brings.

If the Fire was a passionate call to action, then it will fail and people will not be swayed by it—the flames here have no fuel, and they blow themselves out in the breeze. Similarly, a plea to a lover to abandon common sense and run away on an adventure will also fail. Look at Air's example and think rationally instead of being driven by urgent needs.

This can often represent the failure of an attempt to change mental plans into physical actions. You had an idea, you wanted to excitedly run with it, but... the time isn't right. This doesn't have to be a negative outcome. The idea could need more work at the planning stage before it will be ready, or the uncooperative impatience of Fire might have been an unwelcome addition to your calm plans that you never wanted in the first place. Either way, this combination's message is that rushing into things before they're ready will not help you achieve them. You need to be smart and use your mind to check the possibilities before opening them up to the world of fast action.

Sometimes this reading can also mean an abrupt ending, where the forces of Air that cannot be appealed to emotionally will cause a snuffing-out of a bright situation. If the Fire is due to go out, then use this in the most positive way that you can; take the opportunity to see it clearly with the intellect of Air, and order your thoughts to make the best outcome.

While a lot of these situations sound negative, this reading is frequently positive. The angry crowd will see common sense, the loud lies of an agitator will be seen as false and ignored. Air resisting the angrier parts of Fire is an extremely good outcome in many cases!

If you desperately wanted the Fire, then be aware of what it takes to build one that will last: earthy fuel, dry conditions, planning. Don't run in before it's ready, and use any setback to build a better one.

# Greater Water over Air

## The Storm

Clearing the mind and washing away the previous situation

...........

*Black clouds and furious rain, with no land visible beneath.*

MUCH LIKE THE reading for Greater Fire over Air, this combination shows intellectual detachment being broken by a huge rush of emotion. In this case the feelings are watery (traditionally more associated with sensitive emotions than Fire's aggressive courage), but when a wave this large crashes into cold reason, the overall impact can be just as powerful.

This is a storm, not simply because Water and Air are fighting it out, but because undergoing a change toward this much Water influence (when it specifically takes away Air's clarity and calm decision-making) will feel like being tossed by giant emotional waves.

Washing away the mental plans you made can cause a lot of fear and uncertainty but it sometimes brings great benefits. Water is adaptable and will not be denied. It can bring love, quench our thirst for emotional connection, and push down old barriers we no longer need.

It is usually challenging, though. Water requires bravery to truly venture into. This particular combination of moving away from the dryly logical Air to the churning emotional depths can be hard on anyone who isn't prepared for it. The key is to be adaptable, like Water. If a situation you thought was academic suddenly affects you very personally, don't fight it or waste time denying it.

Emotions are not the enemy and you will benefit from being truthful about your own.

Water has healing and softening properties, compassion, love and understanding. As this reading shows, feeling these is not weakness but part of being alive and human. It's also part of being a good human instead of a detached, cold ruthless one. When this much Water influence enters a situation, especially as a storm and causing disruption where it maybe wasn't expected, Water can feel like something unwanted or negative. It absolutely isn't negative by default. Even if we are upset about something, the fact that we care (that we can care at all) makes us better people and turns the experience into something valuable.

The physical image of Water over Air is that the raging storm or giant wave is crashing onto ... nothingness. There are no stone walls to wash against or urgent fires to put out. This reading could therefore signify throwing emotion into the air or sky, and wasting energy.

Swapping strong winds for equally strong waves happens when we think we can live our whole lives using only Air. Look closely at the parts of your life you have been trying to keep numb, or explain away using logical decisions when in fact you should be honest about the emotional impacts.

# Lesser Water over Air

## THE SOFTENING HEART
Tackling sternness and sharp control with caring emotion
...........
*A gentle rain high over green hillsides.*

AIR HAS MANY positive qualities, but can traditionally leave people detached, unemotional, and thinking in rigid ways. The Softening Heart cures this with gentle love and compassion, delivering a soft rain that dissolves the hard lines of written rules and disconnection.

With its low strength, there is a chance that the Water will be pushed out of the situation by the Air entirely. If this happens, then emotional arguments will find no purchase, and feelings will be ignored. A person will stick to the letter of the law with no thought given to compassion. This is generally a bad idea at any time, because even being emotionally strong to help someone can still be done while keeping compassion in mind.

If the introduction of a small amount of Water influence succeeds though, this can show the gentle giving of emotional reassurance and feeling to someone who is lost in their own mental actions. Air's narrow focus on mental and academic subjects can be opened up to include another person's life and emotions. The key is to provide this soft rain in a way that causes it to fall lightly everywhere. There is no roof of rock or wood to keep it off, only Air's open spaces, and Water is a good element to softly bring Air's focus back to the wider world.

If you need Air's intellectual detachment, then the distractions of emotional water will not be strong enough here to stop you doing good work. They will add a new dimension to it, but it can be kept at a level where you have a clear head untroubled by heartache or conflict. However, if you are trying to appeal to someone emotionally, this can be a sign that you should restrain yourself because pushing too hard in that way will not work. Lesser Water, when it is used to mean nurturing, loving support from someone who is not trying to take over the direction of the whole situation, can still be very effective and is never a bad thing to do. Lesser Water is a quiet, consistent love that will eventually be seen and rewarded.

# Greater Earth over Air

## The Overworked Scribe
Having your ideas take root in the real world

...........

*A young man at a desk, writing with a quill.*

AIR IS SUPERB at creating ideas and intellectual achievements, but not the best at translating them to the physical world. In this reading, Earth comes in and solidifies those ideas into practical solutions.

This most commonly means a big increase of Earth where there was previously Air, and that the positive things linked to Earth (wealth, security, the home) improve substantially according to previously-laid plans. The formless Air transforms into the very real and solid Earth, and (while this can be a loud crash of rock down onto empty space) it is definitely a move toward measurable events happening in the real world, when they were only ideas before now.

One thing to check is that your ideas did not require great wildness or emotion, because you're not getting those. The purely theoretical plans of Air did not become Fire's loud courage or the Sun's success and glory, but instead moved to be Earth's attributes of slower, sensible endurance and achievement. If the Air that is being replaced needed an outcome which was less ordered, it could find itself trapped by the status quo instead.

There is one very negative reading of this situation as well, which is that the Earth coming in and replacing Air means that your airy ideas will not come to pass after all. A heavy quantity of Earth suspended over empty Air could mean a reverse of normality, or the demands of work or materialism making it difficult to think clearly. It could also mean that practical concerns such as money or the home actually deny you the chance to explore wilder ideas or stop you from having any time for study.

Earth's links to money, work, food, and physical possessions usually mean that we can view the element as success when it appears. We can see its presence as literal riches. Sometimes, however, it is the other aspects of Earth, its stillness, weight, and order, which dominate. This could mean that the plans made with Air are totally stopped by inertia, by paperwork or by the demands of tradition. So while we should be happy when something goes from thought into being given solid form, in this case that form can be boringly solid, and if we want the opposite then there is still work to be done to inject more fun into the situation. Ideas that are ready can be translated into solid achievements—but make sure that your physical needs are met so that you have time to keep inventing brilliant plans.

# Lesser Earth over Air

Creating a safe passage where none
existed, carefully navigating a problem
...........
*A thin walkway of dirt over a chasm.*

WHEN HEAVY EARTH is suspended over empty Air, caution is advised. Lesser Earth over Air provides a more careful approach than Greater Earth would, and is less extreme. This allows for the slow, certain translation of a plan into physical reality.

The Earth doesn't dominate, but it fills in a path that creates solid ground where there was previously nothing in place. This approach is safe, but it brings its own hazards—mainly that there is not enough commitment to Earth to ensure stable support, leading to hopes being placed on shallow foundations.

Air is undefeated here, so the amount of Earth influence that is coming in has failed to translate the mental plans into physical form. This could mean "back to the drawing board" to plan again, which could be positive. As long as the plan has not begun, returning to writing would be a very safe option.

There is another more subtle but still positive aspect to this combination, which is that plans that remain on paper can stay true to their ideals (without the temptation of prioritizing money or including compromises that might be needed if they are to manifest in the working world). The Lesser Earth here is not a harsh reality check, but rather a reminder at a time when the plan can still be changed or continued.

In general, though, this is still a warning that the Air beneath you does not contain any support or structure. If you are going to survive it, you need to fly. You need to rely on the Air under your wings to navigate the problem with intellect and good communication. Look to Air for the solution out of this potentially unstable situation.

If you asked the oracle a question about timing of events, the answer here is "not yet." Earth tried to come in and change Air's thinking to something solid that can be held in the hand, and it failed. More work is needed before that can happen.

To look at it optimistically though, Earth is still the nearest element here and it creates the start of a bridge. The process is close to happening, it's just not quite ready. Keep your hopes up, keep your mind sharp, and eventually the change will come.

# Greater Sun over Air

## Clear Summer Sky
Freedom to celebrate life and success in comfort

...........

*A warm and blue sky with a shining Sun.*

AIR HAS NONE of the emotions of water, lusts of fire, or rich material comforts of Earth. When the Sun comes in to replace it, this potential hollowness melts away in its warm gaze. The sky now has a bright, hopeful Sun in it, and we're free to celebrate the joy of living.

All the aspects necessary for a celebration will be provided, and it is time to relax and take a deep breath in the warm sunshine. Celebrating is important business, especially when you're coming from a place where feelings and emotions weren't the priority.

If you were asking about the outcome of a specific event, then this combination gives easy, happy success. It can also be a message that you need to take time away from overthinking and just have fun—realize that the passing of time means that days off are to be treasured and valued, not put on hold until later.

Don't dismiss this reading's potential for healing, too. The Sun was often associated with Air, and the pairing gives an outcome full of health and a happy heart. The Sun brings out your true self in a strong and vibrant way, and all of the mental attitudes that come with confidently connecting to that just add to the effectiveness of its healing power.

A shining Sun with nothing to block it can extend its reach all over the land. This can bring success, reason, and healing, but it can also give you nowhere to hide. The Moon may give darkness to cover those who act against society's norms, but at midday there is nowhere to shelter from the truth, or from the expectations of others. The Sun helps with this to an extent though, dissolving the rigid blocks of bureaucracy and law with a momentum for rightness to prevail and the right person to gain their place. Where there might have been hardship or a focus away from material things, there will now be a warming influence of health and comfort.

Most of the readings with a Greater Sun are overwhelmingly positive. This one doesn't have a raging Fire or mysterious Moon to wrestle with, but it warms and brings success to the mind and thoughts. This means a happy and forward-looking mindset! Relax and enjoy the sunshine.

# Lesser Sun over Air

## THE EAGLE'S NEST
Gentle healing, lots of space,
and fresh breezes to clear the mind

...........

*A nest supported by tough branches on a mountain peak,*
*with a view of a large valley and strongly blowing winds.*

THE AIR IS triumphant here, and the Sun is reduced to a lesser player within the environment. The height of the Eagle's Nest means that there are refreshing winds all the time, and the far-off Sun is a secondary concern. Its beneficial rays are supportive and healthy, but it stays back while Air remains the stronger influence.

The Sun's presence, which brings success and joy, ensures that this reading is safe from the possible negative aspects that Air can bring when it is allowed to be extreme. The daylight shows us the land below, reminding us that we are not so detached from others or the planet. It warms us, giving some of the physical comfort that Air can lack.

This is a very relaxing reading. There are no walls here, only open spaces and refreshing breezes warmed by sunlight. There are still dangers to watch for, however: don't give in to the temptation to revel in the freedom of the hope-giving sunshine to the exclusion of important daily concerns. Air is good at making plans, and the Sun is good at seeing them through to success, but the Sun did not triumph here. It's a relaxing environment precisely because not a lot is being made to happen, so you mustn't be complacent if your goal was to make great change.

The sunny mountain peak is a wonderful retreat. This restful place is meant to clear your head and allow you focus mentally, but be careful not to retreat into more physical comfort or take yourself away from others for too long (being a hermit can be refreshing, but you should keep looking down to activity on the valley floor as well as up to the vast airy sky).

The conditions for making great things happen soon are very good here. You have excellent visibility of all that is going on, and the Sun helps with this by bringing a small amount of revealing light. An eagle in its nest can look out over the terrain around it with sharp eyesight and swoop on anything it needs to. Air's keen and decisive intellect is still the biggest force present, so use the calm time to make plans for your next step. See what you want to reach out and grasp, clear your head and then decide how to proceed. The conditions are very favorable, but the time for massive change isn't here just yet.

# Greater Moon over Air

## THE ECSTATIC
Magic and mystery break through doubt
and over-thinking; joy, awe, beauty
..........
*A smiling dancer with their head
thrown back and eyes tightly shut.*

THE MOON'S WILD, mysterious energy comes in here and dominates Air's mental clarity. This reading shows a move from clear logical thinking to mystical night: planning and rational decisions are put aside in favor of instinct and revelling in joy and beauty. In combination with Air, one of the least emotional elements, the move to Moon's primal emotion is even more noticeable.

If this change isn't managed well, it can be very disorienting. It could signify a loss of the senses, a lack of mental precision, or even a break in contact with reality.

However, there are many positive outcomes to this as well. While the Moon is not often linked to making solid changes in the physical world, it does touch the inner world of people in a direct and authentic way. Air is excellent at clear-headed communication, but none of that ensures that other people will respond in the way that you want. Touching their emotions can be more effective.

This reading very often suggests prophetic dreams and thoughts, and these should not be ignored. It can also relate to the move from book-learning to a magic that is directly experienced.

The Moon's link to cycles gives this an interesting shape. Air can be formless, or pointedly focused on a single direction, but is nothing like the repetition of the Moon's phases or the circles the Moon weaves around the Earth as they both circle the Sun. This change therefore suggests a lot of movement—not the fast charging forward of Fire, but a move between the shadows and pale light. When the Moon becomes involved, something will always happen, because it is constantly shifting and the matters it deals with are too strongly felt in our inner lives.

At its best, this change also shows mastery—moving from detachment and logic to working by instinct and intuition, from other people's words to feeling your own answers within. To succeed you should let go of dry facts and give yourself over to the surge of mystical feeling.

This is a reading with a huge punch of energy but also enjoyment and self-knowledge. Abandon yourself to the wildness of inner knowledge, and trust that intuition if it conflicts with what more sensible logic would demand.

# Lesser Moon over Air

## The Touch of Silver
The rational is given a small touch of magic

...........

*Moonlight shining through a window onto lines
of black-inked script in a book that is open on a desk.*

Moon and Air are not very similar in character. Air deals with issues you can see clearly and use good communication to describe precisely, while the Moon governs the ever-changing play of shadows over our unknown nights. Sometimes, however, these two forces can combine in harmony. Here the sharp and determined mental achievements of Air are given a softening shine of moonlight. Academic projects will have a little humanity added to them, and those who sit in lofty towers looking out over the land will be reminded of the beauty we can choose to pursue.

The potential prize of these two mixing in gentle ways is to imbue any work with a magic and power that will excite and connect with people. In particular it is an excellent sign for taking magical actions with a clear head. It is also good for giving some romance and magic to a situation you thought was fully known and unemotional.

The danger of this combination is that the Moon is only lesser. Air's logic and disbelief can still stop the full fruition of dreams. An inner connection (to a feeling of the divine, or to ourselves) would go unheard over the reassuring clarity of Air.

On the positive side, that clarity is still present. This pairing gives the wisdom that the Moon can bring without having to abandon yourself in order to feel it or understand it. It is a gentle and useful amount, to remind you that the mystical aspect still exists.

If this is about relationships, it's a sign that you can afford to dream a little without losing yourself in illusions. Search inward for the answer to mysteries, but be reassured that Air's clever, sharp sight is ready to make good decisions less clouded by emotion or turmoil.

If it's other matters then this is a move away from keeping things purely in the mind and an indication that you should put more of yourself into everything. Remember that the Moon is present, not just Air's dry logic, so instead of keeping things purely in the mind you can safely put more of your real self into everything.

Look for ways to add a shine you will be proud of to any aspect of your day.

# Greater Air over Fire

## Conflagration

Explosive increase, massive energy for success

...........

*A fireball, intense heat and sound obscuring all other details.*

AT FIRST GLANCE, this reading could be the same as "Lesser Fire over Air"—Fire being defeated by Air, the candle being blown out. However, this oracle relates to physical processes just as much as traditional correspondences, and in this case the action of feeding an existing Fire with a strong supply of the Air causes it to burn even hotter.

When we take the raw willpower of Fire and channel it through the focus and sharp direction of Air, the results can be devastating. To go into a project with passion and energy and refine your focus with intelligent decisions can lead to great success. Any enemies would do best to run away from this combination. This is the reading for people who know better than to "fight angry," and who keep control of any anger with a detached determination. It is extremely effective when facing others who use Fire alone.

Using this Air to modify Fire without any of Water's compassionate emotion or Earth's grounding caution means that you can easily take things too far. It can bring catastrophe, with results far exceeding safe limits. Don't reject the Fire too much though: with so much Air energy, you can lose sight of the initial reasons you felt so excited for a project and give away momentum, or you can be too detached and make decisions that are too harsh. This is the tightrope you must walk, that by starting with Fire and introducing Air there will initially be a great increase in strength and heat. If you keep adding Air, however, you will eventually blow out your Fire and be left only with clear sight and intellect but no passion or fast movement to drive it along. Greater Air when it conquers can mean moving to a more clear-sighted place of discerning choices, but it can also mean whirling thoughts that fly out of control in every direction. Greater Air offers little help to put boundaries on thought, preferring to provide unlimited space in all directions.

This combination is a weapon and should be timed carefully. It is a little too explosive to be controlled, so you must use judgment on when to stop throwing mental energy at it. A little (even a lot) can be very productive—but too much will remove all the heat that was there in the beginning. Keep it loud instead. Look at the parts where a calmer mind is useful to defuse unwanted aggression, and then keep the rest of the passion.

# Lesser Air over Fire

## The Bellows
Measured control, creation according to plan
..........

*A bellows in a blacksmith's forge,*
*slowly coaxing the coals to the correct heat.*

THERE IS NO chance of the Air in this combination blowing the Fire out completely. The Air is restrained, directed, and the timing of adding it to the mix is chosen to help the Fire achieve a goal.

Just like bellows used in a forge, this combination tells us to apply our brains to a task in a steady way so that the end result will be bigger and brighter. It's work, but work that involves repeated, careful mental effort. Don't lose focus to emotions, but keep the delivery doing exactly what it is meant to.

This reading can show someone who is there to help, to add good decisions to a passionate cause without raising their voice or causing the hot Fire to break its containment. This might be you unselfishly helping, or it could be support that you receive from others.

At the lower end of the Air energy, this can be an approach that is too timid or conservative to give the best results. Allowing the Fire to overrule Air unchecked just lets it quickly flare out without enough oxygen. A skillful artist can increase and decrease the size of the Fire according to their plan instead.

A specific meaning that often applies to this reading regards fiery words and stoking anger. If you have a passionate message to send, tempers or willpower that need to be enflamed, then using

Air's communication to do it will increase the Fire. Air's vibration covers speaking and singing, its mental powers cover memory and having a plan for your speech: bards, singers, and those who want to reach to the hotter emotions of the audience have always used some of Air's aspects to do it.

This combination will not work for reducing the Fire. If that is your goal, then the Air is not strong enough to stop the flames dominating. People caught up in Fire are not willing to listen to cold logic or the most sensible plans. Focus instead on finding a way to reach them through Water's emotions, or ground them with Earth's solid security.

Sometimes pushing ahead with Fire without listening to the intellectual facts of Air can be a good thing—it makes change happen, and prevents getting trapped in inaction. Just bear in mind the bellows only ever make the heat increase and the end result needs to be handled with care.

# Greater Fire over Fire

## THE DRAGON'S BREATH
Incredible energy and determination,
ever-increasing speed and heat

...........

*A giant roaring cloud of flame, with a*
*scaled eye and jaw just visible to one side.*

FIRE IS THE element of the magical will, the passionate intent that powers action. Its hot energy is doubled here, producing continuously more flame. Obstacles are blown aside, challenges attacked directly with overwhelming force.

Fire is one of the fastest elements, and here the sprinting person gets the second burst of energy they need to increase speed even further. In fact, this can be a very supportive reading ... if what you're looking for is lots of raw strength. If you wanted subtlety or some quiet time to relax and think about things, then this is not the place.

There's a great deal of movement, but the nature of Fire is ragged. Much is lost to the sides as more power is poured into the central thrust. With no other influence to direct it, this reading's aim is rough and dispersed—unstoppable, but unfocused.

When enthusiasm and commitment are this high with such a lack of caution or boundaries, it can be difficult to use safely. Be sure that your aim stays true. This is a charging horse that the rider only just keeps control of, a dragon that is more powerful than you.

The ride will, however, be lots of fun. It's an adrenaline-filled rush with so much heat, noise, and light that it will remind you why you get excited about things in the first place. There is no room for overthinking, doubts, depressive emotion, or rational sensible choices. This ride will lift you up, give you power, and help you make an impact.

It will definitely cause great change as the old is burned away, and if that is your goal, then this reading is very clear that it will happen. The will is there, the energy is high, and barriers will be broken.

There is no more detail or direction than this given in the reading, however, so think about which parts you want to ensure remain in the next stage when the smoke clears.

And if you didn't want maximum noise and change? Well, take steps to reduce it. Look at how you could defuse the situation with Water's cool understanding, Earth's stable foundations, the Moon's contemplation. Redirect the flame and make it less ragged with Air's sharp direction. If the problem is a source of anger, realize that more anger will not make things any different, only double the issue.

The Dragon's Breath has potential for great joy and freedom. Look carefully at the alternatives before jumping up to ride in it.

# Lesser Fire over Fire

Being outclassed by a stronger
or more experienced opponent
...........
*Two figures, one confident in power
and the other tentatively learning.*

TWO STRANDS OF Fire have confronted each other in an aggressive way here, and one of them does not have the strength to succeed.

This is not a contest of Air's knowledge or Earth's endurance. Fire represents the hot emotions running through our chest, the courage and willpower to attack, and the very personal reasons that we are motivated to such strong action. It is linked to the core of what someone wants, and a competition involving Fire will always be personal instead of academic.

When Fire and Sun compete elsewhere in this oracle, the interactions between them are very much about levels of expertise and mastery. That is not the case in this reading, though, as both opponents are the same element, but the challenger is simply not as powerful as the target. They might have fewer people on their side, or less determination, but they are using the same tools.

Depending on the question that was asked, this failing newcomer might be you or someone else who cannot compete against you. Obviously this combination is good news if you are the lower element: the Fire that the new influence cannot overcome.

However, it is also possible that the Lesser Fire is someone who wants to help and chooses to use less strength, being restrained enough to do good without seeking glory. This doesn't work very well with this element because Fire is too concerned with action and their own inner needs. Where Water can represent an extremely varied set of emotions and qualities, Fire's emotions are mostly those that do not lend themselves to teamwork easily. So in this case, the second person who is deliberately trying to help in a small way stays as a minor addition to the main process, because any bigger involvement would cause conflict with the main person involved.

Merely wanting something is not enough to secure it for you. Fire alone, going up against more Fire, can fail in a confrontation of strength. The answer is to look at all the other tools available: the other elements, emotions, and less direct routes to the goal. This can be hard to do when you're already moving forward with heat in your chest, so if there's a subject where you're sure you're already correct, check your options again. Do it especially for those areas you don't think you need to. Look at the barriers you could come up against, and don't take for granted that they will be overcome.

# Greater Water over Fire

Defusing a situation, escaping or preventing
danger; adapting successfully to a threat

...........

*A large wooden bucket of water tipped over a small indoor fire.*

THIS IS THE reading with the most obvious physical interpretation. Water being of enough quantity to overcome a fire is the classic image of neutralizing a danger.

Of course every combination has other aspects to it as well, such as those purely related to the magical correspondences. In this case that would be primarily about the emotions.

Although the physical picture looks on it as a danger, the element of Fire does not have to be negative at all—it can be a life-affirming passion that drives our heart and mind, a burst of courage and energy to get things done. Fire gives us heat and light in the darkness, power for vehicles and warmth in our muscles. While the extinguishing of it is not necessarily bad, be careful which aspects of Water are brought up as a result, since they can frequently contain not just loving care but also often unwanted emotions, such as melancholy and jealousy. When these act to destroy the existing passion and drive, this reading becomes a situation where negative emotion prevents progress by causing doubt and sadness.

Of all the pairings possible in the oracle, this is one of the most beautiful. Fire and Water are different to each other, often opposed, frequently shown as red and blue. They are not Earth's static endurance or the Moon's mysterious distance, but instead something that we can experience in our daily lives—capable of movement with changing edges that flow together and react with energy. This is a meeting of opposites that promises to make change happen.

That change could be very good. Fiery emotions turning into Water is a superb transformation for love, where losing the initial heady lust can let strong loving emotions rush in to replace it. Being a peacemaker, a loving friend, or partner, choosing to be understanding instead of the giving in to the hot righteousness which can sometimes lead to hate—all these things are positive for you and the people around you.

The replacing of Fire by Water might look at first glance to just be an end to the danger (and fun) brought by Fire, but as we've seen here it can also be a lot more: an end to conflict, preventing a threat before it causes harm, or a return to compassion and care. It can be a near miss, an avoided danger, but only if you move away from Fire yourself and choose to explore the situation using Water.

# Lesser Water over Fire

## THE DIPLOMAT
Placating another person, soothing a situation

...........

*Steam rising from damp clothes over a fire.*

BRINGING ONLY A small quantity of Water to a Fire is a risky strategy. At its best it can reduce the flames in an acceptable way while keeping the fuel burning efficiently. Miscalculate, however, and it will simply hiss and be boiled away by the superior heat.

Lesser Water suggests a range of emotions that Water represents but not those that feel too big for us to manage—grief, black depression, or other overwhelming feelings. These are missing from Lesser Water, which is often instead the application of gentle caring or support in a way that isn't too distracting from the main element's task.

The Fire needs to be understood fully. If it is too hot for the amount of Water, the new influence will fail to divert a plan from its course, and soft words will not be enough to prevent anger.

The Diplomat walks a delicate path. They have chosen not to dominate, but this gentle approach allows for failure unless the message can be presented in the best way. If you are the Fire, then listen. Water's contrasts and compassion bring wisdom to the plan that you're pushing through with heat, and you won't lose any momentum by considering the new and positive things Water can bring.

So listen, but don't automatically assume that the Water is correct or that Fire's properties are negative. Fire gives us courage, makes change, and puts passion into hearts. It provides heat and light to lift our mood when it is dark. It cooks food to help us eat. Water has failed here, and that could be a good thing: Water is an element that contains more darkness and deceit than most— a shifting, unknowable bringer of healing but also of fears and strong emotions. Powering through its uncertainty with a brave Fire will accomplish a lot.

This combination often means "Bravery defeats fears ... but listen to your friends." The Water will not overwhelm you or put out the Fire, so it does not hurt to take notice of it and to value it. If it is someone offering advice, then you can trust that they are sensible enough not to stop the main direction of things, and skillful enough to put their words in a way that will not disrupt your wants and needs. If your question was about a friend's Fire, then you must be the Diplomat: be calm, and do not look to escalate any arguments. Seek an entry through gentle emotions, not clever thinking or making your own light as bright as theirs.

# Greater Earth over Fire

## THE TREASURY-KEEPER
Preventing danger by having sensible plans,
creating order and wealth

...........

*A powerful, imposing person with a*
*heavy cloak over wide shoulders.*

WHEN A FIRE is smothered with Earth, the heavy, dense material drops upon it and prevents any air from reaching the source. This is also the action that the Treasury-Keeper takes when faced with a request from someone too angry or reckless: denying it with great weight and finality. As the person with the responsibility for guarding their leader's money, the Keeper needs to be certain, sensible, and unbending, and Greater Earth provides rock-heavy stability to enforce this.

If the Fire was an unwanted danger, then this is a good act by someone with the resources and will to achieve it. If the Fire was passionate hopes or another's willpower, then the application of Earth's mundane, grounded reality could be a cruelty.

The triumph of Earth here is a return to the status quo, but that is not necessarily bad. It is a safe and fertile place to begin new ventures from. The Treasury-Keeper rules over the vaults by being prepared and secure, traditional, and careful. This does not lead to any wild new discoveries, but it does give a stable place to begin from once again.

Look carefully at the benefits of using Earth. It is strong and supportive, enduring, patient, but also green and full of life. It is good for us, provides food and shelter, and gives order to a cha-otic world. Within its grasp are jewels and precious metals, crops, and fields that reward work with wealth.

We can be attracted to Fire because of its bright flickering light, but we need to remember that its high speed and hot burning power are not always best for us. It's true that this combination shows a slowing down from quick Fire to still Earth, but this can be positive too. A safe place to rest is important.

Someone with the knowledge and power to put out the Fire just did so—there are a lot of situations where everyone should be grateful for that. Alternatively, if what you wanted was to make a lot of change, and what you're getting is stubborn inertia, then start again from the beginning. Find a new Fire and let this guardian keep a brooding watch over the area they have claimed here.

# Lesser Earth over Fire

## WOOD FOR THE FIRE PIT
Careful fueling bringing comfort,
order, protection, and the energy to continue

...........

*A small fire in a pit, with thick branches at its base.*

THIS IS ONE of the most harmonious readings in the oracle. A warming Fire is fed with gentle amounts of fuel and things proceed in normal order. Cooking and heat are provided to the household, and comfort and prosperity are increased.

The magical correspondences of the element of Earth are more than just the strength that comes from dead weight of rock, they also include the growing things of the Earth, such as trees and wood. Here, an existing Fire has a small amount of wood added to it from outside and flourishes because of that new fuel.

If the goal was for Earth to dominate the Fire, then that has not happened and the existing plans were fed instead of being stopped. But this feeding is not catastrophic, and even a small amount of grounding Earth energy is beneficial to most situations.

The Fire triumphs here and Earth fails, so it's quite possible for the Fire to rage out of control in this situation without the proper soil or stones as a barrier to keep it in. Although this sounds dangerous, it can be good—if the Fire was in danger of failing, quenched by Water or outmatched by the Sun, then the wood keeps it alive and thriving. This could apply to sexual relationships being rekindled, or signify that passionate causes will not run out of momentum and fail.

If you were trying to put out the Fire, then Earth was not the way. The slow, respectable inertia of Earth has been rejected, or part of it used to make the Fire burn even brighter. Look instead for ways to bring Water or other elements in to reduce the flames. If the Fire can't be defeated at all, it can still be manipulated: changed by Air or the Sun, with the Sun being an example of how to be purer, better, with a higher purpose.

The presence of Earth means that this Fire is usually a stable and reassuring one, and this combination provides a happy background for any new choices to be made. It is a reading of great comfort, and of the mundane needs being taken care of so that you can turn your attention to the matters most important to you. Your Fire has not been stopped by the typically heavy, immovable forces around you, but has instead used their intervention to progress and move forward in a useful way. If you are tiring, new fuel will come to keep you going. If you wanted to reject the Fire, then this is an opportunity to look again and reassess it for all its positive contributions.

# Greater Sun over Fire

## Knighthood
Passion becomes success;
recognition over your peers, glory

...........

*A leader standing on the left of the image, with a large yellow Sun behind them. They face to the right and knight a kneeling student by touching the student's shoulder with a sword.*

SUN AND FIRE are closely connected, but red flames cannot hope to match the brilliance and power of the blinding Sun. Here they have nevertheless been judged worthy, and the Sun's success and glory descend onto the Fire. What started as a small goal a person felt passionately about has been visited by a blazing Sun.

By moving from Fire to Sun, this combination deals with an increase in both volume and purity. The Sun has many correspondences that link it to higher ideals or greater achievement than the Earth-bound elements involve. The quality of its flames are different, the color and intensity of its light are more refined than the smoky fires we make from wood or other common fuels. It is also much bigger in size and reach than anything we could encounter in our lives. With the Sun's gifts of success and health, this is a very positive reading.

This is generally not a confrontational pairing (as some Sun and Fire can be). Fire has not tried to usurp the Sun, and the brighter presence brings great success to any endeavor that doesn't require the cover of darkness.

Sometimes, however, the Sun represents a person who is not the reader, in which case its presence could steal the successes of the other, drowning out their Fire's light with the Sun's own. If this is the case, then there is no fighting it—the Sun is a master and the Fire cannot begin to compete.

The way to avoid this is to ensure that you are the Sun. If your activities are currently linked to Fire, then make sure that you also keep higher ideals in mind. Don't be unthinking, selfish, quick to anger, seeing only your own cause. Don't get caught up in the journey or the excitement of movement. Look at how you can elevate your actions so that they benefit everyone instead. Look at the decisions you are making and see if they are being compromised too much from the ones that would bring a more glorious outcome.

A knighthood isn't a sudden change—it's not something that is given one day without the consideration of the day before. A Knighthood is a recognition of the superior character that someone has already shown. It is a growing and purifying of the inner Fire. If you want one, look carefully at what you could do to deserve it, and start doing more of that.

This is a visit from an honored guest who bestows fame and achievement. Be honorable in your response to it, and you will be greatly helped.

# Lesser Sun over Fire

## THE GUILDMASTER

Skillful assistance from an expert source

...........

*An older person sitting before a shining round plate,*
*which has six joined segments each made of a different metal.*

HERE THE SUN arrives quietly to lend its skill to Fire. Being immensely older and more powerful, even with lesser strength the Sun effortlessly outperforms Fire in any endeavor, but now it decides to restrain itself. What could be overwhelming is deliberately and humbly held back.

This is a major exception to how the energies in this oracle often work, because a Lesser Sun still outranks the existing Fire (instead of the typical action of lessers, which is to either fail in their attempt to replace the existing element because they don't have enough strength or to deliberately only exist in small quantities to help the existing element's cause). This Sun is lesser but still stronger, choosing to be benevolent as it extends its help to one who deserves the assistance.

If angered, the Sun could still (without even having to resort to becoming greater) effortlessly outmatch the Fire. It would become a more skillful opponent who wasn't even trying, yet would still succeed. This isn't the default position of this reading though, because the Sun has come in with a nonaggressive lesser strength.

This Sun is wise. It has seen the Fire, knows it could have replaced it, and decided that the task Fire is doing is important and must continue. That is something to focus on: if the situation is

Fire, then you should not fight against that but instead support it. If you already believe Fire to be the best approach, be reassured that someone with higher wisdom agrees with you.

Acknowledge that there are people out there who know more than you do and accept their help. The result will be much grander for it. This Fire needs a touch of the golden Sun, and whether that comes from you or someone else, you should look around to find it before assuming that nothing can be improved.

There is a second way to read this combination. While the Sun cannot be lesser because it wants to be stronger than Fire but fails, it can still be lesser because it is not the right time for the situation to move from Fire to Sun. This is one of the few cases where the lesser strength can signify the Sun saying "no." It is choosing not to replace the Fire.

The Guildmaster's symbol contains all of the elements, because mastery requires more than just staying inside the skills you already know. The Sun could use its superior knowledge to see that another element is needed here and then act to block advancement until the right answer can be found. While it contains success and perfection, the Sun is the element that is least concerned if another route is taken to reach it in the end. It is an endpoint, a glorious finishing, and although it is strongly linked to Fire, it sees the other elements as well. So the first definition to consider is that the Sun is gently lending Sun energy to help the Fire situation, but the second is that Sun is refusing to let the project move to a Greater Sun at this time—and the answer to that blockage is to look at more than just Fire for your next step.

# Greater Moon over Fire

## MAY DAY

Primal magic, wild attraction, celebration

...........

*A green field with people dancing around a large bonfire,*
*beneath a huge Full Moon the size of half the sky.*

THIS IS SUCH a fun reading. Fire is unpredictable, high energy, excited, and not very disciplined. Instead of being a grounding or focusing influence, a Greater Moon is a blast of otherworldliness and magic. The natural impulsiveness of Fire is whipped up by lunar energy into a delighted and wild celebration.

The Moon's cold remoteness does change the energy of the Fire a little, but only to give it a connection to ancient magic. The message of this combination is to cast aside the sensible chains of work and duty associated with Earth, the precisely guided thoughts of Air or the possible melancholy or delightful distractions of Water, and revel in an intensely strong inner connection combined with Fire's adrenaline.

This will of course lead to you having complete impatience with mundane tasks and responsibility. That's tough, because when the high energy of Fire meets the greater aspect of another element, the result is often bigger than both of them, and you can only hang on and hope for the best. Greater Earth could slow the Fire down, Greater Air could demand more focused thinking, but the Moon does not impose those boundaries. If anything, the Moon removes barriers, especially psychic or religious ones. The Moon loves light and won't reject the firelight even when other greater elements often seek to dominate or erase the previous existing element. The Full Moon doesn't: it is distant and approves of the generation of light. It is not merely adding a small amount of silver to the situation, but demanding—from a place that is already Fire—that you remove any walls to inner wildness.

This is a glorious, joyous reading that can be scary in its intensity but is worth throwing yourself into to see where it goes. It is one of the most powerful for magical or religious work but has a loud and quickly-moving feel, perfectly suited to activities that wouldn't be allowed by day. If there are taboos it would make you happy to break, then this gives permission. If there are people you want to celebrate with but who cannot be reached when restrictive traditions or the spotlight of society's attention are on you, then this combination is the time to seek them out. The only rules are those belonging to the Moon at night, with heat and joy beneath it. If you are honest about your inner truths, this pairing gives the energy to follow them and surge over barriers.

# Lesser Moon over Fire

## CANDLE MAGIC

Success in small projects, blessings for
personal needs; subtlety bearing fruit

...........

*Three beeswax candles burning brightly in a clearing at night.*

WHEN THE LESSER Moon met Air previously in this oracle, it opposed the dry, logical aspects of Air's academic correspondences. When it meets Fire here, again as Lesser Moon, it simply lends a light of a different type to the current flame—a filtered silver that adds a small touch of magic and possibility.

The Fire's progress is unaffected by the new element and it can burn steadily to achieve its original aim. The Moon brings a connection to deeper things in the process and allows for a move away from science and toward magic. This is a good reading for dearly-held personal projects.

The Moon's light does not affect us in the same way that the Sun's does, even though they are linked. It is seen by night—a time when the land is blanketed in darkness and the Moon is the only potential lamp. Since the lesser forms of the Moon include those it wears when it is a thin crescent and also when completely dark, in other combinations it can even include the possibility of a covering cloak of darkness to hide under.

Here though, that darkness is pierced by the Fire that survives. The changing Moon can be seen, but does not dominate, and its silver light adds to the activities of the Fire. Be sure to take notice of this subtle moonlight even with the brighter main Fire burning nearby: being blinded to the possibility of adding wonder and magic to a project because of Fire's more familiar light will leave things much less varied.

In particular, this combination lends itself to pairing Fire and magic or mystic feelings. Candles, charms, and quiet prayers for deeply personal causes are all empowered by this. Fire's emotions are ones we feel strongly in our chest: conviction, courage, things that we believe in to a burning level, not just casually. It inspires us to strong action, fast movement, making change. Any prayers that come from it are felt from the heart. They are certain and urgent. The Moon brings a cool relief to this and lifts our concerns to a higher level. It is something that moves in cycles but promises to return, and so it allows for answers that don't need to follow the accepted routes.

The new influence of the Moon should not be rejected, because it is not at all threatening in this situation. As well as being lesser in strength, the Moon's light is just light. It has no physical form like Earth to affect the burning of the Fire, only an added beauty. Embrace that, and look for it. Don't lose yourself in contemplating the distant white orb, but hold tightly to the Fire and feel your needs urgently. Take solace that there is more out there, but don't move away from your original goal.

# Greater Air over Water

## THE CONFIDANT
Sensible advice, a person who is
outside of the emotional upset

...........

*Two figures seated closely together,*
*talking and holding hands in a comfortable way.*

WATER'S HOLD ON our emotions make it the great element to represent love, anxiety, or conflicted feelings about a situation that feels too big to escape from. Where a lot of Air influence could enable us to see something clearly, being in the middle of Water's murky, changeable currents can make it feel as though we never get enough breathing room to stop worrying.

This is where a good friend comes in. They have your best interests at heart, but their view isn't clouded by the same emotions. The new person has a clear head so can assess the situation and choose the wisest course.

Since the new element is greater, and is therefore replacing the current one of Water, it's possible that you could be the Air here. Abandoning Water's dreamy emotions for Air's quick and clear thinking might be just what is needed, and going forward with the sharp sight and calm intellectual decision-making is often a relief after turbulent waters. If you're looking for relief from unwanted emotion, Air allows you to regain the space you need for making decisions.

This new influence could easily manipulate those who are already more emotionally involved. Staying rational, detached, and calculating means that you are not swayed by personal preferences or hesitation. Intellect is the way to find the superior answer here (or at least the most effective route to it).

The historical benefits of a swift breeze over water gives this reading an additional meaning of fortune for journeys. This wind over waves does not bring the disruption or chaos of a storm, it is not the same as the strong pull the Moon has on the seas, but instead is likely to be purely beneficial. Water is a good foundation to be blown along the surface of by a sufficient wind, and Air's fast incisive movement is a lot more effective than Water's dragging weight.

This reading suggests that the head wins out over the heart—the clever decision will be made, and communication won't be hampered by too much emotion masking the issue. If you are looking for advice, or next steps, the answer lies in time spent deliberately thinking on it from a place outside of the push and pull of watery feelings.

# Lesser Air over Water

## THE TRANQUIL LAKE
Peace, calm, leisure; safety to ride with the current
...........
*A still surface of a lake, waves lapping gently against the shore.*

BEAUTY AND PEACE reign here. The waters are not stirred up by winds, but remain clear and calm. No challenges or tensions are created and there is time for rest. If you are navigating the waters, they support and move you without argument.

Generally there is little to worry about with this combination. Relax, take a break, and wait for the next change. Use the time to explore and reconcile your emotions. It's true that with no wind in the sails, you may be unable to gain momentum. However, you can rely on the current of the Water to keep drawing you on at a relaxed speed. The slight breeze does help you to keep a clear head and breathe easily without disturbing the waters.

Lesser Air could be seen as failure, meaning that the situation was not changed by clever thinking and instead remained in the more fluid realm of slow-moving Water. Comforts and emotions were too strong for purely intelligent appeals to win anyone over.

But *lesser* also represents the less forceful properties of Air: instead of intellectual arguments and long-sighted plans, which could impose themselves over the influence of another element, Lesser Air concentrates on the communication and conversation that carries on the breeze. It gives pleasant music and speech without rousing passions.

Lakes have sometimes been seen as gateways (particularly to an underworld). When a lake's surface is calm, it is safe to explore. Air has been rejected in this reading (or forced to be gentle), so Water's connection and inner communication will be the important aspects.

Take the time to appreciate this leisurely pace and safety. Ensure that you are making space in your day for real relaxing—not just time set aside, but having a relaxed mind as well, free of distractions or guilt. Take time to check in with your inner needs, the passions and wants that don't always make themselves known when we're busy.

Water is an element strongly linked to health but also to confusion and illusion. Saltwater purifies and cures while fresh water nourishes us, but down in the darker depths there are still monsters. Exploring those depths regularly is essential. Using the quiet times to really face up to what is challenging us emotionally can be the way to make a lasting inner peace.

If you're currently needing a break from the fast pace of life, this reading is a blessing. It is time away in a gently bobbing boat on a still lake, with a breeze bringing scents and murmurs from the land around. If you're looking for answers to a personal question, then this lake becomes a gateway—a door to be opened bravely. The contents are not Air's ideas or logic, they are deeply-felt emotions and the things in life that sustain us. Don't make decisions to ignore those emotions. You will discover that there are treasures hidden deeper that you can only find if you keep looking. Relax, and let truths bubble to the surface while your environment is serene.

# Greater Fire over Water

## The Invincible Flame
The determination to succeed against all odds
...........
*A roaring bonfire flame with no*
*visible fuel, suspended over a vast sea.*

WHEN FIRE COMES into a situation and finds nothing but Water all around, and yet still goes on existing and triumphs in overcoming the water, that flame will never die. This reading is the classic example of success through sheer willpower and drive.

Emotionally, we find these two elements once again splitting a range of possible feelings between them. Water covers love, but also all the cold, dragging grief and pain that comes from heartbreak. Fire has lust, attraction, and hot determination. Here it drives off the negative heavy emotions with fun, passionate energy.

There are dangers to this as well. Fire can be destructive, angry. The Water being driven away could have been compassion and love, losing out to the short-sighted burning rage. Regardless, this Fire refuses to be extinguished. Whether it is friend or foe, you must take notice of it in any plans. It sustains itself without fuel, it does not weaken, it is sure and determined.

Fire and Water coming together to the result in Fire's triumph also represents technology. Steam turbines and trains harness the power of these two elements (which cannot exist together) crashing in combat. In some pairings of elements we can see the final relationship as still allowing some form of each to exist in the new way. This isn't true for Fire and Water: they fight, and they do not coexist except during the time that one of them is being changed. That is where the connection to steam is seen, in the temporary and dynamic generation of a new form of Water, which will itself disappear soon as well. That movement and energy can be transferred to our own uses and the conflict drives progress.

A defiant flame existing on a lake of water and flourishing despite the hostile environment is a source of great power and determination. It doesn't care what others think or whether they believe it can succeed. It will succeed through willpower, courage, and high energy.

If you feel that your cause has no hope, no support or resources, then this reading says the strength of your will alone is enough to keep it going. If you are already struggling, this becomes a rallying cry to tell you that you will succeed. Eventually the landscape will change to only contain the Greater Fire, as all the Water is driven away. This means change to everything except the single-minded purpose the Fire has.

To succeed, make the Fire your own (or alternatively take steps now to stop it—and not using Water.) Assumptions that traditional ways will slow its progress are wrong and shouldn't be casually relied on. It is invincible.

# Lesser Fire over Water

## The Nymph
Flirting, plucking at the emotions
...........
*A smiling, cheeky spirit of water and fire.*

FIRE AND WATER mix harmoniously here, with the emotional equilibrium of Water raised to excitement by the small but persistent flame. Any attempts by the Fire to incite anger or battle will fail through lack of strength, but the surface of the waters will be warmed and cheered by the effort. Love will be acted on—not with hot lust, but sincere and merry kisses.

This is a warm and happy reading. It allows Water to retain all of the loving emotion but adds a pinch of fun.

Be careful not to reject the advances. Water left cold can mean a person unable to lift out of depression, or wallowing without moving forward. Instead, seize the fun moments that life brings every time they are offered. Fire's warmth and energy is a gift we should accept whenever it appears.

Taken to extremes, this can also be somebody refusing to be made angry or violent but instead staying true to their feelings. Staying in touch with our watery side is a healthy, caring place to work from, and Fire's adrenalin-filled call to action is not always wanted. Fire is fun to be around. It's noisy and bright, and life would be boring without it. This doesn't mean that we should give in to its demands every time that they appear—our days would be loud but short if we did. Water's influence is valuable; it keeps families together and allows for peace, compassion, and contemplation. Using it as a shield against Fire is often a good idea.

A Lesser Fire is a dancing candle flame here, kept safe in an environment of caring and emotional Water. These elements together are always a little bit insubstantial since we don't have an image from our daily lives to picture them like this. Earth has edges, the Sun is a circle, but it's difficult to imagine how Water and Fire hang together in space without others involved. This means that the combination of them has a sense of constant movement and change—when they are paired in the oracle, something is happening and things will have fizz.

Look at all aspects of love and relationships, and think about the small actions you can take now to have fun with them. This is a very sexual reading in a frivolous and joyous way. It is a warm bath emotionally, but with a flickering light drawing you forward to new things. The cheeky Nymph has a smile.

# Greater Water over Water

## The Dreaming Sea

Mastery of dreams, careful steering of deep tides

...........

*A person asleep with their eyes closed,*
*breathing peacefully under the surface of the sea.*

WATER IS CONSTANTLY changing, unknowable, and less than solid. Any combination where Water is the new element has a chance to change that shifting energy, but this pairing more than doubles the amount of Water involved. The element of dreams, feelings, and illusions is mastered here with the dreamer fully engaged and in control.

The way to gain this mastery is to become one with the subject of your attention. Water permeates barriers and defies attempts to grasp and move it in conventional ways. You must learn to flow with the hidden currents, ride the swells, and use the immense power of the Water itself instead of imposing any plan from the outside, which goes against its natural style of movement.

To do this you need to put aside the lists of questions from Air or the impatience of Fire. Water will move when it is ready, and it has its own deeper currents. It cares more about feelings than details, and this pairing will certainly bring a lot of feelings! Greater Water crashing over the land is a hazard, but over more Water it means that you will be safe if you abandon your shelter and swim. There is no choice about this—Water is the way forward and you will only find answers by submerging yourself completely.

This can lead to a lot of crying and a lot of feeling emotion very deeply. It can also bring unparalleled wisdom and power, inner peace and creativity as you dream new ideas into being. Dreams tell us truths and inspire us to things that don't yet exist—they let us play in delicious tides of love and fulfilment.

It's important not to assume that the wisdom revealed this way has been translated into the hard-edged waking world yet. There is the chance that you could be lost in delusion with no solid ground to build on. Keep swimming. The end point will become clear, but only if you head into the deeper waters.

The Dreaming Sea is a journey, involving the discovery of things that aren't always seen up at the surface. It uses feelings to let us go deeper than we're used to and shows sights we wouldn't understand if we hadn't traveled to their own land to see them.

If you wanted an answer that wasn't Water, this reading says "No—it's more Water!" The only response is to shrug and dive in.

# Lesser Water over Water

## The Rain on the Lily Pond

Emotions nurtured, gentle happiness and refreshment

...........

*Raindrops disturbing the surface of a pond,*
*with green leaves and lily pads floating on it.*

WATER CAN BE a challenging element, and when it is disrupted by another coming in great strength, then the upheaval to emotions can be severe. This reading doesn't do that—instead it soothes the water with a light rain. It reassures us that the emotional connections are the right ones to pursue, and provides its own caring touch.

This reading dissolves away barriers and provides a peaceful, restful environment for healing. There is no heat or forbidding walls, only the calming sound of rain on water. Yes, you will get wet without the shelter of Earth or the heat of Fire, but a pleasant rain in a calm environment does not need to be fought against. Embrace the caring properties of Water. With no solid ground, there is no choice but to go with the flow and appreciate the beauty that is given to us.

If someone is feeling particularly vulnerable, then it's true that there is no shelter from even this light rainfall. However, the message is one of support: the emotions you are already feeling are valid, and by providing a pleasant supportive scene here, the Lesser Water is ironically giving you the strength to look forward and find a new element next. There is only Water in this picture, but the new influence has failed and is lesser in strength. This means that trying a different one now could be more successful.

The most pleasant way to enjoy the music of raindrops and chirping frogs in a lily pond is to be ... under shelter, right next to it. The rain is beautiful to look at as it hits the pond's surface and the green plants, but it's even better when you're seeing it from somewhere dry. Earth is therefore one of the best elements to move to when your world is full of Water. A mountain made of tough rock is not swayed by joyous or sad emotion and doesn't quickly change its course if there is an obstacle. Building ourselves a shelter out of Earth can help to soak up excess Water and give a good foundation for moving on to future things.

The key is to endure and take solace from the well-meaning support of the new gentle Water here. This is not an unpleasant place to be, and the rain has to stop sometime. While we gaze out over the pond, we can be refreshed and become ready for the next challenge. This is a place of safety but also a reminder that if you want things to change, you need to put solid foundations in place to make it happen.

# Greater Earth over Water

## THE RESERVOIR

A fortunate supply of help, nourishing
roots, a friend who aids growth

...........

*Healthy soil over rock, with channels of water*
*rising through it to nourish the plants at the surface.*

WHEN GREATER EARTH provides a solid field of rock and fertile soil over the Water beneath, the Water becomes a hugely positive influence, feeding and healing the life on the surface.

When your mundane concerns are currently slow and stable, then reaching down to explore refreshing waters can be very enriching. There is a lot about this reading that points to enrichment in fact: all the Greater Earth results can be seen as the subject of the situation moving into being made more physical, linked to work or the home in a very real way. From Air, ideas become reality. From Water it is feelings and emotions, friendship, and healing that becomes embodied in the physical world when it had previously only been in your heart. If this is about the workplace and earning money, then it comes from a project that you care about personally. If it is a situation in relationships or the home, then again it moves from a base of good feelings into a more reliable and physical manifestation.

The only danger here comes from Earth's heaviness—it can be boring, predictable, and reliable. This is all brilliant most of the time, but if you were hoping for more Water or the frantic speed of Fire, it could be slower than you wished.

If the Greater Earth goes to extremes, then it could prevent the Water from rising up to aid the green plants on the surface. This could lead to the crushing of dreams beneath the unyielding rock, and practical concerns denying the needs of the heart. Do not become solely focused on efficiency or safety in work or home life, instead allow the opportunity of safe, nurturing emotions to come gently to the surface against a solid and reliable background.

The Earth reassures us that our plans have good foundations, and lets the (sometimes unpredictable or messy) water be contained and drawn up for its positive aspects. The Water truly is a reservoir to be called on, but all around is dependably safe ground, capable of fertile growth and sheltering support. Look for opportunities to turn the things that you care about into something capable of supporting you. Look at the people around you who you could make a more solid part of your life, but hold on to the emotional connection as well.

# Lesser Earth over Water

## Quicksand

Out-of-control emotions that
are not grounded enough by reality

...........

*A dangerous pool of quicksand, unmoving but deadly.*

WHEN EARTH ATTEMPTS to overcome Water but does not have the strength to do it, the result is often disastrous. Water's flexibility is not the ideal base to stand important matters upon. When it comes to the long-term security of the home, work, or wealth, Water's emotional and changeable reasoning is rarely the right answer.

One solution is to use more Earth in the future—keep pouring on the rock and soil until the danger from Water is contained or overpowered. Be dependable, predictable, make and follow plans, be calmly strong. Water's wild emotions can be too powerful to handle without some grounding influence, and this message says that Earth attempted to add solidity ... but that it failed and the result cannot be trusted.

Quicksand has just enough Earth for the ground to behave like a liquid. Mudslides and earthquakes are also ways in which the usually dependable ground becomes less fixed. You should be very careful that the amount of Water in this situation is wanted.

It's possible that it is. Maybe you need deep dreams, wild emotions, and to lose yourself in love or feeling right now. In that case, the Earth here is the mundane world that has tried to drag you back—but it did not succeed. This is a victory for dreams over a predictable daily life that wants boring safety.

Often, though, this situation is a trap. Quicksand is one of the most obvious warning combinations, because Earth influence brings useful things like money, food, the home, order, and stability. These are not ideas that you can do entirely without for very long.

Regardless of how you feel the balance of elements is playing here, there is danger that should not be ignored. A change needs to be made or the chance of failure will be too high.

Water wins over Earth and remains the main situation after the defeated newcomer retreats. You should therefore look carefully at which aspects of Water you will be facing. The unpredictable, changeable liquid nature can leave you lost and confused if you don't give yourself some more solid ground to stand on. Dreams and feelings are good, but if you want them to manifest in the real world, then they must transform into solid achievements. Check that you are suitably grounded and that your emotions are not overruling common sense.

If your emotions are perfectly calm and you decide that more Earth is what you want, then keep going. The situation is still fluid, but there is at least some Earth here, and adding more will only firm up the ground to a safer level.

# Greater Sun over Water

## The Sunny Shore
Physical feeling, joy, health, leisure
..........
*A blindingly bright beach of golden
sand and blue water, with a strong sun above.*

THE SUN'S POSITIVE, health-bringing influence is strong here, and since it is greater than the existing Water, it does not allow for Water's murkier or less enjoyable emotions to make themselves known at all. Instead, the scene is given bright light and enjoyable heat. The Sun can be warm, but it is not beating mercilessly down upon dry ground in this pairing because there is no Earth—only Water instead to provide pleasant relief.

If you are asking about any situation at all regarding love, friendships, or feelings, a Greater Sun is one of the best elements to move into. It represents glorious success and happiness. Any "Should I?" questions have been answered here with a resounding "Yes"!

There are many cycles in nature, but within them must be times when the Sun is highest in the sky and you are at the beach in summer. The older days of work and worry have been paid, and this is now a time for leisure. Ice will melt, blockages will be dissolved, and warm success will follow instead.

This can be a very intoxicating effect. It gives a bright, positive rush of success and reward, and it feels good. There is a chance of being blinded by the constant shine on the water (and losing yourself in thinking that a life of leisure is all that matters), so remember to keep hold of the important things and not give in to decadence. Going too far into vanity or seeking personal glory could spoil the things that you previously gained from the Water. Water frequently involves other people, so keeping them in mind instead of caring only about yourself is a good way to stay grounded.

Another way to explore this is to look to the spiritual aspects of the Sun. It is not common firelight but something purer and more refined that speaks directly to us from above. The constant light brings health and joy and illuminates every dark corner. This can help you to keep your focus and let the truth come out. You'll have good information to work with due to its influence.

For now, take some time to relax and celebrate as needs are met and happy emotions rule. There is warm weather, cool water to drink, clear ocean to swim in, and a reliable, hot sun above. Keep your gaze away from the brightest light and remember to stay connected to whatever Water there is so that it isn't driven off entirely by the heat. Celebrate that Water moving toward success.

# Lesser Sun over Water

## DIAMONDS IN THE STREAM
Glimmers of brilliance, gentle
contentment, treasures to be found
...........
*A running stream of clear water in bright sunlight, with the
tiny crest of each ripple in its fast flow set ablaze by the Sun.*

THIS READING IS one of restful beauty. A stream drifts quietly,
with the sun reflecting in the gently moving peaks of water. It
is not too hot or too bright, and the lazy flow causes a feeling of
great peace and calm.

The diamonds also represent treasure held by the shallow Water.
This can be something that has to be reached for, using your hand
to break the surface and search for prizes, or alternatively a wealth
of good feelings and contentment that should be sought within
yourself.

Water is the primary element here, so the Sun's aspects of success and achieving goals are not as strong as Water's possibility
for dreams and fragile illusions. You will have to work with the
stream, breaking its surface gently, if you want to keep the shining gold that it sweeps along with it. There is no quick ending to a
situation here. Nothing is resolved yet, but the waiting is pleasant
and it's a good time to seek out the rich prizes on offer.

The Sun can be quite demanding. It is rejected here, trying to
take over but eventually yielding to the Water. This tells us several
things: that the situation governed by Water is not yet ready to
move into successful recognition from others, that we don't need

to worry about any of the potentially negative aspects brought by the Sun (it does have some, being traditionally associated with male power and laws), and that we should look more closely at Water for what it could contain that is worth keeping. It's easy to think that a move toward Sun is always good since the amount of success it represents is large, but let's also value the unique things that the original Water brings.

In our world where conflict and aggressive gain is made to be so normal, it can be a good thing to behave in harmony with Water's empathy, friendship, and caring instead. To have another influence move in on that but still hold strong to the Water is also a valuable lesson. Feelings and emotions do not make a person weak.

The Sun in small amounts is very positive with no great challenges. It brightens and gives beauty to everything it touches, and when it does this to Water, the result is especially remarkable.

The scene here is one of great beauty and promise, the finding of treasure or unexpectedly good things, and a reminder that small peaks can bring bright flashes of insight and contentment.

# Greater Moon over Water

## THE GREAT TIDES
Nature moving in harmony, cycles
...........
*A Full Moon, pulling on waves of water underneath.*

THE MOON'S ENERGY here is huge, and its influence is felt by the oceans. The tides go out and roll back in, creating opportunities for life amidst the movement, and in this way nature is providing healthy cycles. In balance, these are healing and restorative.

Out of balance, this scene can be a blazing Full Moon above a thrashing, stormy sea. Every regular cycle has its extremes and moments which do not fit the expected pattern. On a normal night, the Moon will pull in the expected way. Anger it, or increase the energy massively, and it will become a shining floodlight above furious waves.

Both the Moon and the Water change constantly. This means that the natural flow and ebb of events promises that any extremes must always return to a center eventually. If you are looking for hope that change will come, that there will be movement brought to a situation or that it must finally leave one extreme position it has been held in, then this combination says it will.

The Moon is also strongly linked to our inner psyche, and the tides it pulls at are not only those of the sea. A Greater Moon in this oracle is a big event that cuts through our defenses and is felt keenly in our innermost selves. When paired with Water, the outcome hugely affects our emotions and powers. This is a superb and crashingly powerful reading for any psychic or magical workings. It provides a dark sea under bright moonlight, constantly moving depths filled with fears and feelings, and connection to the deeper parts of the mind. There is almost no logic here and no time for detached reasoning or control. It is instead about intuition and empathic contact, feelings and the revealing of mysteries under the Moon's knowing glow.

From full phase to dark, through all the shadows in-between, the Moon does not provide instant answers or solid ground. What it does promise is change and secrets (and those can be just as needed). It is not the Sun, using light to show the sharp edges of things to the world, instead it hangs above a dark landscape of shadows and illusions. Nevertheless, a Greater Moon is a steady and bright light and paired with Water it will shine that light into the feelings and intuition that we keep under the surface. Do not try to grab for straight lines, hard edges, or solid ground. This is a rolling sea you must float in instead. You must commune with it and sink into it. Take the time to do this, because the answers to your questions are not obvious and cannot be found by looking outside, only inwards.

# Lesser Moon over Water

## THE STILL SOUL
Inner silence, focus, and serenity
..........
*A misty Moon behind clouds,
hidden and hinted at by its light, over still waters.*

THIS LESSER MOON is present above the waters, but not in a strong enough way to be influencing them. It is not totally visible, and that absence is peaceful. What is left is a still and silent scene of gentle waves at night, with a diffuse and foggy moonlight above.

This is an opportunity to look within and discover what your intuition tells you when there is no distracting influence. The Water allows you to connect to the truth of what you feel, both emotionally and in your blood, your innermost instincts. It is not pulled off-course by the Lesser Moon, but the silvery influence does gently lift the activity to a sacred level.

This stillness and peace is very sought after and difficult to achieve, so make use of it while it lasts and pursue it if you are not yet there. Create the quietness and undisturbed space you will need to look within, to hear your inner voice without the outside noise. This is the pairing of meditation, of the ending of anxiety, and a restful and beautiful inner landscape.

This kind of inner searching isn't easy. We cast this oracle asking for solid answers, and this combination more than most refuses to give any. It has no connections with achievement at work or at home, no journey to explain how others will react to us. It is about ourselves, and peacefulness, and stillness. Frustration can make our attempts to get to that place even more difficult!

But it's not a total stillness. The Water of our inner landscape is a moving thing, and the Moon is a shape-shifter hidden by cloud. We are not using the Moon's magic directly here since it is lesser, but the glow from it being nearby is enough to make our work with Water into something special.

Other people are not the answer to this reading. It says that your answer is about you alone, and that if you want to find truths you will have to cut away the distractions and talk to your deeper self. The exact means of finding serenity to do this can be through any number of actions. It does not have to be unmoving meditation: it could be dancing at a loud concert, if that is what takes you out of your head and away from the noisy fears which normally stop your true beliefs. The answers you are looking for will only come when you can connect directly to your feelings without the demands and fears of the outside world.

# Greater Air over Earth

## The Shaking House
Bringing freedom to a stagnant situation
...........
*A downstairs room being battered*
*by outside winds, items on the walls rattling.*

EARTH'S HEAVY SOLIDITY is overcome by superior winds here, which can be both liberating and scary. Air brings many benefits: freedom from constrictions, knowledge and far-sight to quickly make decisions, and an escape from tradition and duty. It can bring better communication and knowledge through writing, speech and thought, and leaps of intellect.

But Air's movement is quick and unpredictable, changing direction in a moment and whistling around obstacles. When it is greater than the Earth influence, this freedom knocks down walls and lets ideas leap about in new directions. There is not a lot of security or comfort in this chaotic movement!

Earth's heavy rock is dependable and durable, its change is slow and careful. Moving away from this is not always pleasant, so it is important to concentrate on what is gained: the ability to make intellectual connections, to rely on logic and facts instead of just following what has always been done, to embrace the freedom of soaring above instead of building fortifications.

If you have been feeling trapped, this will be a chance to leap ahead thanks to mental ingenuity. Confining walls are blown away and the mind is free to move. Losing the heavy chains of Earth in favor of taking to the skies is a thrill, and keeping the solid Earth beneath you is much more stable than having an element suspended over Air or over Fire.

Several combinations of the elements show ideas taking physical form, but this does the opposite. It moves away from reliable, dependable structures and shoots up into the air letting thoughts and speech escape into wild flight. Having the Earth below could have meant that this adventure is made safe, but the move to Greater Air is so large that it is more appropriate to think of it as the Shaking House. Big things are going to happen, mentally. If you think outside the usual limits, throw yourself into furiously overthinking the problem and stop keeping the answer connected to money or home duties, you can let it go wherever it wants in the open space without thinking of the eventual real-world consequences. This is important for the process of inventing new answers, but be aware that Earth is the weaker element here, signifying a possible loss of the things it provides—don't let home, career, or money stop your thoughts, but do check afterward that the ideas you reached haven't totally cut you off from support.

If you've been feeling confined or trapped then these winds will blow down the walls and bring freedom. Our minds are not limited by what is happening to our bodies or in our homes. This is a reading of chains being broken and soaring freedom gained.

# Lesser Air over Earth

## SEEDS BORNE ON THE WIND
Successful fertility, nature working
to aid all things, gentle fresh air

...........

*A view from high in branches, seeing seeds*
*blown toward fertile brown soil in the next field.*

THE ELEMENT OF Earth represents not just unmoving rock and metals, but also the many plants and trees that grow as part of Earth's fertile power. Green shoots and healthy crops rely on the life in the soil and the sustenance of the land.

When the Air lends a gentle hand to this process, it scatters seeds and leaves to new ground. The Air itself cannot overcome the Earth's solid foundations but it can add its travel and speed to the existing Earthy aspects.

This is tremendously powerful for fertility, and signifies the healthy rhythms of nature and the relief of a refreshing breeze among the trees. Tradition and traditional movements will not be denied, but their fruit can be depended on in the future.

Since the Air is lesser, this is a reading of keeping your mind on the prize. You mustn't get lost in mental distractions, empty talking or overthinking. The treasure here is the element of Earth, which represents mundane but important matters, and you should "stay grounded," remembering how valuable the home, work and food on the table is.

You should also concentrate on your body. If your mind is racing, you can help to stop it by eating, drinking water and sleeping.

Take care of your bodily needs: move to a different room, leave the house, walk for five minutes, and see new things.

Air's presence here does mean that thinking is not totally the enemy. It hasn't taken over as the main element, but it is still part of the picture. Earth is often linked with the idea of farming: doing work now and seeing the rewards later. Air's influence takes the seeds grown previously and distributes them to new fertile ground, but with gentle breezes instead of a strong disruptive wind. It helps with a breath of fresh air, stimulating the mind and allowing communication to bring about the rewards you are due.

This light breeze won't be enough to move the situation away from the expected—there will be no quick travel to new places, but ideas will be heard and the plans laid for new beginnings. Logic and well-reasoned arguments can start to bring life and movement to a stubborn situation. Just be careful not to reject the home comforts in favor of what theoretically looks like freedom.

Since Air tried and failed to be the new situation, look to Earth for the answers instead.

# Greater Fire over Earth

## The Forest Ablaze

Clearing the way of obstacles, destroying
the status quo to allow a fresh start

...........

*A raging forest fire, trees consumed by tall flames.*

This is a challenging reading. There is great energy and destruction, a breaking down of the existing order to make a new way. When trees burn in a forest, the ground is enriched—but left with no cover until the local life regrows.

Large, aggressive change is wrought here by Fire on the aspects of Earth. This can be violence, destruction, or simply a high amount of angry, passionate effort overturning the established order. This reading means that change is inevitable, and that it may look like disaster, but that the cleared ground will be all the more ready for rebuilding afterward. Sometimes bad routines are so entrenched that only wiping the board clean can force them away. At other times, this great change can be unwanted but must be faced. The land will survive, and the foliage will return without neighbors to compete with for the available sunlight.

Fire is important to us. It is our urgent inner need that we hold to very strongly and will defend with passion. Overcoming the inertia and old traditions of Earth can be a positive thing in many situations anyway, but doubly so when it is to move to such an important new place. The transition itself is usually difficult, though.

Large change tends to bring the thing that you want, but because it is so big the boundaries that can easily grow to include other people's wants as well. It can be scary, and feel like it is moving out of your control.

On the other hand, we have to be realistic. There is no life without change, no excitement, and no hope for the future. Change is your friend, even when it means a risk to the reliable structures of home or work. Where Earth is often slow and bound by rules Fire is a defiant shout. It's a rebellion, and set of demands that things must be better.

This change is coming, so either be part of it or take cover until it has passed and fight against it afterward. If you are asking advice on how to do something, the answer is "burn it to the ground"—make big change. Don't only do half or go into it with low energy and no motivation. If you're going to make something new, make a noise about it! Try to make the best, brightest version that people can't help but notice.

If you're scared about a big change, then start making plans now. The future is not fixed, and anything that changes can be altered again later. If you don't like this one, make your own once it has passed.

While it's frightening, the Greater Fire can be a force for great good if you ride it. If there is a New Year's resolution you've talked about but never done, a change to your routine for your body or career that you would make a real difference, look into it. Greater Fire is one of the few elements that has the power to finally overcome the heavy weight we feel holding us back to the usual way of things. It's a chance to make a real difference.

# Lesser Fire over Earth

## TENDING THE CAMPFIRE
Responsible care of home comforts and security
...........
*A well-kept campfire, with neatly stacked branches and a*
*secure perimeter so that it cannot burn outside its confines.*

FIRE IS A useful tool. It warms us, cooks our food, and provides light at night. When it is kept at low levels near the home, it gives great comfort and service. This reading shows the benefits of combining Earth with a small amount of Fire. The Fire brings energy, movement and drive, while the Earth keeps things secure, safe, and grounded.

Fire makes change. Relying too much on known and safe places can hold you back from new experiences, but the carefully tended flames here make a useful torch and heat source so that you can explore at your own pace.

This is a reading that means "comfort," saying that your needs will be met and your home will be warm. It has a strong link to the protection of the home, and the rejection of the chaotic change that Fire can bring. A sensible foundation and controlled exploration is a very good way to do things—don't leap ahead, just keep moving and the support of Earth will keep your feet on the ground.

The problem with comfort is … it's boring. If you'd been hoping that the Fire would break things up and lead to change, then it has failed. Earth is crucial for providing the things we need, but it's also slow. Stones don't run, mountains aren't known for unexpectedly changing direction. If you see Lesser Fire unable to overcome Earth, this means that inertia and stasis was too strong for change to happen.

This can be great news, of course. There are many times when we want events to stay as they are, we want just a little bit longer to prepare before trying something new. If you're asking "should I do this now?" then it is saying "not yet." If you're asking what to do or how to do it, the answer is: look after yourself first. Make sure you have fuel for the fire, cooking, and a safe grate around the fireplace so that it stays small. Listen to the needs of your body and concentrate on taking the actions that will leave you rested and secure.

When the question involves other people, this pairing could mean that someone else is trying to disrupt your calm established order, but they will not succeed. You can see their brightness from the safety of your well-prepared dwelling, and you should look for a way for you both to coexist safely. Fire is useful in the right amount and the right place. Earth is critical for life, but food can still be improved with a cooking fire. There is no great danger here, so use safe surroundings to plan for riskier times.

# Greater Water over Earth

## The Deluge
Emotion and vision triumph
over blockages, healing replaces stasis
...........
*A huge wave flooding over a wide
expanse of cracked brown ground.*

THIS IS A reading where every property of Water succeeds. The connection to emotions, to healing, to vision, to daring and dreams comes to the fore and replaces Earth's rigid rules.

As with many of the Greater Water readings, this flood can be difficult to control. Earth's hard structures do not keep the water out in this case, and any stability is lost in a wave of emotion and receptive change. When there is an amount of water this large, it does not care about details and takes no prisoners—it will flow into every space, surge over every wall. There is no choice about dealing with it, instead it must be acknowledged (and it's probably a good idea to go with its momentum).

This is one of the readings most focused on romantic love. It takes over every other concern here like a great sea of loving emotion. Feelings are reciprocated and grow strongly and quickly.

Immersed in Water, we are gently supported and transported to a different way of moving and thinking. Instead of the security of brick or wall, we have a new medium that we share with other living things. It provides, cleanses, heals, and helps us travel. The trick is to stay afloat or make dives within your capacity and hold your breath.

Being "in over your head" in such a wave can actually be very healing. The world is going to send something your way, and it will move you and carry you to new places.

The potential negative aspects of this are really obvious though, and when they come in at the expense of Earth, they can be quite disruptive. Losing Earth correspondences means a reduction in stability and also in material possessions, wealth, and security. If you're tempted to make giant emotional decisions that leave you vulnerable at home or at work, take the time to ensure that your material possessions are safe while they happen. Do the boring things before going on a wild adventure—especially if you're enjoying yourself and don't think you need to. Stop, check in on the routine tasks that keep you stable, and then enjoy the ride afterward with the confidence that you're not forgetting anything.

# Lesser Water over Earth

## THE RAINS

Happiness and good fortune;
the crops are watered, the earth refreshed

...........

*A light rain falling on brown soil and green plants.*

HAPPINESS! THIS IS a very positive reading indeed. Soft rains nourish the fertile Earth, and all of the life in nature is renewed. Water lends its best qualities (gentle nurturing, cool relief from any hot temperatures, healthy purity) to the domain of the home, security, wealth, and land.

Of course, there are always those who do not like the rain, who in a light shower will resolutely stay inside and wait for it to pass. A very stubborn person will be unmoved by emotional appeals here and refuse to see the beauty in processes that bring bountiful life at the expense of a temporary inconvenience.

Those with wisdom will enjoy the emotions for what they are: the stuff of life, watering the green plants and giving gifts to the home and family. There is no negative effect on the amount of Earth in this reading due to the Water; it is compatible and in a small amount, which is always welcome. The Earth is still the main element and only benefits from the lesser presence of the Water.

Earth's soil receiving the rain leads to health and growth in a stable environment. The element of Earth is used in magical work to "ground" strong forces—to neutralize and bury them, much as a lightning rod directs the charge harmlessly into the land. Water on its own also neutralizes in this way, washing things clean and purifying. The mix of both of them makes this reading absolutely superb at moving on from old influences, burying past grievances and healing.

It's also a positive reading for talking about the current moment. You would think that rain means sad times, but here they are soaked up by the ample Earth and used to refresh and grow all the life. It is an act of renewing—absorbing the moisture to prevent the ground from becoming dry and cracked—but in amounts that do not wash away the soil. Water's potentially turbulent emotions can overbalance us when we are standing on one of the more changeable elements, but Earth gives us the secure foothold and support we need so that the small amount of Water is only an enriching addition to our lives.

Finally, this reading suggests that it is just the first step in a reward that will come along at a later date. The crops and plants are watered so that they will grow, and with the good healthy ground as a base in this pairing they are sure to bear fruit in time.

# Greater Earth over Earth

## THE MOUNTAIN
Protection and resilience; a safe fortress,
calc emotions, an imposing presence

...........

*A towering mountain of brown rock,*
*seen from ground level at its base.*

THIS IS A reading of great strength and endurance. A shield of
hardest rock and solid foundations, the Mountain is invincible.
It doesn't move and it cannot be harmed. You can break swords
against it, use words against it, but they will achieve nothing.

Nothing shakes the Mountain. It can provide total protection, but
only by remaining static. It is immune to emotions, fun, pain, and
fear and doesn't take part in any of those. It endures in patient safety.

When danger is near, the Mountain can be a good shelter for
a short time. We must remember though that we are not made of
stone—change is inevitable, and we would not be alive without it.
This invulnerable rock is a place to retreat to while we catch our
breath, but not something we can take away to use elsewhere. If
we refuse to leave its shelter, we will be trapped in one place.

Earth's aspects are unopposed here, so any of them that you
seek will be very present. This reading also often refers to strength
and stability in areas associated with other elements, such as love
and relationships.

The most common message from this reading is around imme-
diate feelings and it advises us to get our shields up. Be the mountain: stubborn, proud, defiant. Be tough, sure in what you want,

and unwilling to move. If you do these things today, you will be invincible.

Earth's solidity can be helpful in succeeding over doubts and fears, but this is never in a superficial way. We can bury painful things in the Earth and it will take them from us, dissolving their potency with its grounding magic. When we apply this strength to our own bodies or hearts, then the shield of rock we put around ourselves is not brittle or lacking in care for others. It does indeed make us invincible, able to divert Water's woes and the Fire of enemies, keeping us sensible in the face of the Moon's intriguing mystery or Sun's heady pride, but the Earth influence isn't just an unhealthy numbing of our emotions. It's an understanding of our real roots, strength built on reliable and enduring foundations.

The mountain reminds us that we have a right to exist, and that the things that are already our own are valuable. Its depths contain gold and gems, its caves and rocks are the walls of our dwellings.

This much Earth energy is great for both the home and wealth. It promises that our choices in work will be productive and safe. It tells us that if we sit still and be strong then the rewards will come.

There is almost no movement in this reading. If you are bored by situations in the home or work, this offers no change but reminds you that you take your home with you in your body and self-belief. The best part of receiving a reading like this that does not contain any catastrophic change is … precisely that it doesn't contain that disruption. Remember to value what you already have, and use your supports to stand tall every day in a sustainable way.

# Lesser Earth over Earth

## The Ploughed Fields

Strong beginnings; hidden stability, good foundations

...........

*A cut-through of the Earth, showing*
*solid rock beneath a layer of healthy soil.*

RICH TOPSOIL SITS supported by strong rock underneath. This brings good support to a healthy process and shows a successful foundation for a relationship or project.

A double Earth pairing is always strong and tough, but here the softer soil of Lesser Earth on top is also rich and useful. Both sides of Earth's appearance in the world are shown: the strong resilient stone and the green fruitful fields.

This is a reading of things being in their rightful place and of work already done. The fact that the new element is lesser does mean that there's a chance that a different one might have more success—Earth is not very wild or dynamic, and steady endurance is not the only way. It is a safe route though, and this combination is extremely positive with a solid base.

This is the path of crops and farming, but after the initial work has been completed: the fields were ready and have now been ploughed. They're open to receive the seeds and will be fertile ground for growth. There is no Sun here to make the crops grow very quickly, but the land is perfect and success will come in time.

That does not mean that you should stop working or thinking ahead, however. This a very dry reading, with no Water for the land. It is very slow, with no Fire to move our bodies or Air to dart about with brave new ideas. There are always many opportunities to move more quickly in a direction when starting from a situation of Earth, and this is a good time to look at those next.

The healthy soil has come in and sits in the right place over the stable Earth. This is a combination that should make us grateful for truly reliable ground to stand on. In many pairings the elements might be disrupted as a new one arrives, particularly if it is greater in strength. It could fall into the empty spaces of Air or splash into free-flowing Water. Even if this settles down again, there has been a lot of movement during the interaction.

In this one, Earth meets Earth in an amount that does not challenge the current settled level. It is a friendly element in a useful quantity. We need to recognize when this happens and pay attention to being grateful for the patient support that we receive.

Despite the lack of crashing waves or raging fires, this reading is an exciting one because it says that the groundwork is laid for anything to happen next—and it will probably be louder than the status quo at the moment.

# Greater Sun over Earth

## THE MONARCH
Promotion, recognition

...........

*A crowned noble figure backed*
*by a large Sun, looking down onto a city.*

TO THOSE AREAS typically denoted by Earth correspondences (such as work, the home, money, food, and domestic stability), the new influence of the blazing Sun brings success. It comes in strength and is more powerful than the initial situation, able to impose its will. This nearly always means recognition or promotion at work, or at the very least safety from negative events in the workplace or home. The Sun brings safety through order, something that fits with Earth very well, but does it with energy and optimism. There is almost no chaotic energy in this reading but a high amount of safe and orderly fast progression.

The Sun is blinding and there is a danger that you will be the one caught up in its promise. Too much focus on personal fame can lead to home and work being ignored—don't forget that earthly interests were the original point here, not just you individually. Sudden personal success can spoil the places you rely on for security, especially the home, so don't pursue it or get distracted by it to the extent that those closest to you feel left out. Bring it into their lives too. An unrestrained Sun shining down on the Earth can lead to drought and cracked ground, so keep a watch on the extent of your actions.

The danger to most parts of our home or career is not serious however, simply because of the huge amount of wealth in this reading. This Monarch is rich. Both Earth and the Sun have associations with money, gold, and treasures, and the combination of them both means that anything that would damage your wealth is unlikely to happen.

This is a reading of rewards coming after hard work. It is the farmer being repaid for his efforts with a rich harvest, or the merchant who invested sensibly seeing his profits come in. If you are stuck in the rain, hoping for a sunny day in the future when things will be right, this is the delivery of that promise.

The Sun's links to health are also important here. The Earth is very much about our physical bodies and the Sun always brings life and wellness. In this case, that is physical health.

Overall this is a combination that suggests on the surface that the Sun's success means good things are coming. When we look deeper, we see that this is exactly right: the doubling of both money and health make this a very positive pairing.

# Lesser Sun over Earth

## The Fields at Sunset
Work still to be done, endings and choices

...........

*Rows of wheat, fully grown and waving under*
*a gentle Sun that is sinking to the horizon.*

The Sun here lends aid to the growing crops, ensuring that they flourish. It is not too hot, and does not dominate the Earth, but works with it to enrich and empower the growing things.

Where the reading of "Lesser Earth over Earth" only describes the ground as being ready, this reading is of the Sun's action to make the crops grow right now. It signifies healthy, natural actions proceeding as planned but not yet finished.

The Sun is comfortably warm but not blazing. This lower energy can lead to inertia or complacent behavior at a time of opportunity when you could really excel, but this is not always a bad trade-off. Rather than straining and potentially falling from the height you'd have gained, the gentler Sun ensures steady success.

However, the Sun's lesser strength here is also a serious issue. Success did not come, the task is not finished. The Sun is not at noon but is setting and will soon disappear. It is a sign of endings, and of time running out. This change will happen soon, and ignoring it is not a realistic option.

You have a choice. You can let go of the day and start fresh in a new direction, or fight to turn this Lesser Sun into a greater one. The Sun is not the only element that leads to success and you do not have to keep stubbornly struggling with the same issues to force it back up into the sky: doing so is a very Earth-like behavior! Water would never oppose a problem in that way, it would allow the object to sink as it wanted to and would flow around to the sides instead of wasting energy.

But sometimes, when the problem is to do with our homes or the people in them, we decide it is right to struggle. Time has already been invested and we could gain the desired outcome if we just keep going. If that is the case, then check the work already done in the past and look ahead to the future. Make sure this goal is the one you want to keep putting in effort to save.

The energy of this reading is of the Sun gently warming the Earth. The power of it is not high, so the continuing security of Earth prevails against the promised change that a Greater Sun could bring. This means there is still time—the Sun has not yet gone, and the evening is peaceful. Use the time of contemplation wisely before committing to the next step.

# Greater Moon over Earth

## The Howling Wolf

Wild freedom; ecstasy, joy, adrenaline;
escape from normality; powerful magic

...........

*A wolf at the edge of a forest with its*
*head thrown back, howling to a Full Moon.*

THIS INTERACTION OF the Moon with the natural processes of the Earth links our sacred feelings to the land and animals. Its greater strength here means that the wildness is very high, and the reassuring mundane reality of everyday things gives way to the mysterious, magical power of the Full Moon.

This is a reading of primal power breaking down structures, of acceptable behavior making way for wildness. Despite this, it retains a strong link to the heavy land. It is not "Moon over Fire," two elements that increase the amount of chaos in a reading with nothing to hold them back, but instead is constrained here by the presence of grounding Earth. It breaks the barriers of tradition and inertia but is starting from a point of great stillness compared to the other elements.

The Moon is a very natural pairing for Earth, but in extreme cases the fact that it is specifically overcoming order and stability can also mean that the outcomes feel more severe. Lunacy, madness, wild emotion, the breakdown of reason—all of these are the Moon overwhelming the rational and mundane daily reality that the Earth had brought.

This can be frightening, but it's a natural thing to happen when enough time passes. More than that, it is essential. We need to break rules so that we can see the boundaries, and we need to connect with the primal part of ourselves so that we know what is truly real for us.

This pairing brings ecstatic freedom, and a tremendous amount of power in magical workings. Any work that you do with it will be authentic, touching your true inner self. The Moon is blazing very brightly in a black night sky, and the fields and forests beneath it are transformed.

There is no Fire here, so the freedom is more about the rejection of Earth's sensible and known structures than about giving you the highest personal energy that could be achieved. By moving away from Earth and toward the lonely, haunting mysteries of the Moon, the feeling is often of being extremely ungrounded. If you weren't planning on this, then be careful! It could mean that you should seek out those friends who can bring you back to normality or keep you in more familiar surroundings.

Or you could choose not to. Many people who are interested in divination are those who choose to look outside society's normal expectations. If that holds no fear, then this is an opportunity for exploring in a place without the typical restraints. It allows for personal celebration and connection, for losing yourself in the Moon or being freed from restrictive walls. Just be careful to come back again afterward.

# Lesser Moon over Earth

## THE MOONLIT GLADE

Peace and contentment; natural magic, secure
and calm surroundings; passive resistance

..........

*An empty clearing in a forest, glowing with moonlight.*

THE BEAUTIFUL SIGHT of moonlight over the Earth gives peace
to the mind and security to the land. This Lesser Moon is not
as bright as a Full Moon, so it does not push its influence onto
us by shining demandingly strong over cities and countryside.
Instead it lights the ground with a quieter energy. This creates
more shadows and allows for hidden things, but also gives restful
silence at night without making the Moon's power too frightening or forceful.

When the Moon is a gentle glow instead of a floodlight, some
pairings give a greater chance of losing yourself in illusion or deception. This is not a big risk here, as the Earth's solid and sensible
influence is stronger. With that security from Earth, the moonlight becomes a safe and illuminating background to the nighttime events of man. The way is lit for adventures, and time spent
alone is given a profound and healthy touch of the sacred.

The Moon has long been the patron of thieves and those running from injustice, anyone who needs the sheltering darkness and
shadow. It protects but also relaxes boundaries allowing people to
explore banned subjects and take daring actions. With a Greater
Moon this would be a wild smashing of taboos, but lesser acts more

gently: it chooses to recede, taking its light and letting the darkness back in so that we can act away from the eyes of others.

Sometimes taking the small resources that we have and withdrawing them is the only action we can take. If we are not in a position to influence others, or to exert ourselves with force outside our own bodies, then leaving a situation can still bring change in a way that we can manage.

It is important to recognize the strength of Earth in this reading. It does dominate even though the Moon is here too. The magical silver light shining down onto the mundane daily structures can't make change happen by itself, but it can show us more clearly how unsatisfactory some of those structures are and give us hope for what they could be with a touch of special care. It is a silent torch, briefly showing us a better way before disappearing into darkness.

The Earth is also not the enemy here. The Moon's lesser light gives people the space to leave the city and explore different ideas, but the Earth ensures that they can do it in a safe way. None of this sounds as though it can be easily applied to a caster's question about love or a risky decision: the answer to those is "Earth endures," and that the shifting, tempting Moon can give wisdom from a safe place but should not be run to when the Earth is still available.

Overall, this is a beautiful reading of soft light from a place of security. Unexpected shadows can show you how things could be, or you can spend your time enjoying the mundane being given sacred meaning in a peaceful way.

# Greater Air over Sun

## The Governess

Good guidance, steering the currents to find the best answer
...........
*A stern woman in formal clothes,*
*with a cloudless rich blue sky behind her.*

The Governess is a strict, unemotional teacher who—while entirely correct—can still run the risk of not being caring enough about life.

Air is replacing Sun here, and while that takes away some of the glorious and happy aspects of the Sun, it does mean that Air gets to bring in what it does best: clever thinking, space, and freedom, and the flexibility to quickly change. This means that the new influence is very likely to be the right and intelligent answer, even if it drags you away from playing in sunny days.

The Sun can represent a person achieving their potential, and Air can suffer from being too detached and lacking compassion. There is therefore a danger to watch for here that a purely logical approach could cut someone off from their goals. However, this is also a chance to grow up. The Sun can be arrogant and self-obsessed, while Air's clarity lets you see things as they really are (including the importance of others and the reality of events).

This negative take on the pairing is not the most likely outcome though. More commonly, we see that a challenge is shaped by the Sun, and Air is the correct answer for it. The Greater Air is a successful solving of a problem using lots of concentration and intelligence. It has retreated from the distractions of other elements upon our bodies or emotions, and has managed to devote the time and determination needed to get the answer.

In other words, be smart. Don't assume that personal fame or glory is the best way, and don't be blinded by the beauty of others. Keep a cool head and look with discerning eyes. Be a bird of prey in a vast sky, sharp, quick, staying high above and looking down to see things as they are. Trust in Air to find the best route.

A Sun in the open sky is a combination with no walls: the only clues or blockages will be the subtle steering of air currents to the goal. This time, the Sun is beneath and the empty Air is above it—meaning that either the Sun is too low and is defeated or that our viewpoint is higher than usual and we're flying in the Air above the setting Sun. This is a very distant, lonely place. When we choose Air's intelligent answers over the easily-seen glory of the Sun, it can be isolating. Others will assume that the person who glows brightest is the best, or think that anyone who wants to retreat into books and learning when there's a more obvious success to pursue is foolish. Neither of those statements are true, and Air can give us incredible blessings. Fill your lungs to gain the determination you need, and throw yourself into flying the mental winds to unknown answers.

# Lesser Air over Sun

## The Spring Morning
Good conditions for relaxed
contemplation on personal situations
··········

*A clear spring sky with warm sunshine and cooling breezes.*

THE SUN IS associated with success and happiness, but often in a way that talks about the whole person. It can be of someone achieving their potential, healing because their whole body and mind are in the right place, fulfilling destiny. When we look at what this would feel like in a more relaxed situation, it becomes a warm glow that focuses on the real individual's needs and happiness.

In this pairing, there is no punishing Sun beating down upon crops or struggling Sun cut off by stronger Water or Air. Here a gentle breeze adds to the present situation of the Sun and the result is a comfortable, healthy environment.

Try not to throw yourself into the aspects associated with the Sun too quickly in this reading. There is only a small amount of Air as the other influence, and it will not be enough to keep you away from a hazard if there is one. Relax into it instead, and explore your healthy inner needs while drawing on a refreshing stream of Air. This will give you the intelligence and detachment to make good decisions based on what you find.

Be aware that the Air has tried to take over here and been rejected and use this to look at the negative behaviors of Air that you should not fall into. Since unemotional logic can take you further away from your Sun, make an effort to engage with your feelings and intuition instead of just the pointed intellectual enquiry of Air. It is very easy to lose connection with our personal Sun when we are swept up in frequent or worried thoughts, but that has been avoided here. Air tried to dominate and failed, tried to pull your gaze from the glorious Sun but instead you were able to keep focus: give such thoughts a small amount of time to make sure that you aren't missing anything important, and then return to the wisdom of the Sun.

Both the elements here are quite removed from the heavier and more worldly ones we know. The Sun and Air interact in a place high above our concerns, but that is nevertheless filled with beauty and purpose. Not much needs to change when you are there or when you receive this reading: an end result of the Sun is a great situation. Tempering it with a little bit of Air is often a good idea too, but there is enough room up here for mistakes without danger. This environment is forgiving—there is nothing to crash into nearby and a lot of joyous light to lead you. You already have your goal, if you can see it; explore possibilities using emotion or connection, but definitely not with frantic thought.

# Greater Fire over Sun

## The Runners

Trying to match a master, a close race,
triumphing against a superior

..........

*Two fiery horses and riders, one red and one yellow,
racing each other at absolutely top speed.*

There is so much energy in this reading! The result is a rare thing, a student proving themselves the equal of a master. In human experience, any amount of Fire is always less powerful than the Sun itself, but here it is shown as greater: how do we begin to think about that? It is as though the Sun set a task and Fire succeeded at it. Not any task, but one that the Sun considers its own speciality.

This is therefore a tale of the hardworking student overcoming impossible odds to gain the first place through a high amount of effort. It is not a purely intellectual exercise—with the amount of thrashing energy being thrown around, the task is going to require very hard work. Greater Fire shows that it's on a topic that the person already cares about, something very close to their own nature.

In all situations where a task is this personal, pride and anger are some of the bigger dangers. People can be overeager to rush in and furious at delays. While the main theme is a success against great odds, Fire will at least play a part in how it is achieved: this win will not happen without passion, willpower, and energy.

Racing at full speed against another is a risky business. You could stumble and fall, injure yourself, or strain muscles. On the other hand, it can be great fun. We need peak experiences in our lives, times when we don't worry about what is sensible or about conserving energy for later but go all-out in pursuit of something we believe in.

This win was not achieved by clever thinking or patient waiting. Fire's energy is one of movement, of making change happen, and it fills our chests with a shout. It's sexy. It's also really, really reckless unless you remember to take precautions as well. The relationship between the elements here mean an unexpected win, but it's difficult to see that in isolation from the amount of heat that is involved.

If your question is about the time to do something, the answer is "right now," as fast as possible. If it's about whether it is wise to do something... that's different. This is a reading of proving the impossible, of competition and incredible success. It can represent a situation which looks too difficult to achieve, but says that you will do so if you bring enough energy and determination. The first thing you should be thinking about is that there is danger written all over using this much Fire. You need to burn brighter than the Sun—it's entirely possible that you can't do this if you just try to get conventionally hotter using up your own resources. Consider getting help and preparing yourself. The stakes are high, so put everything into finding the way that will show the experts that you're at their level too.

# Lesser Fire over Sun

## The Prodigy

A wise student, capable of skill
and restraint, first steps in a new project

...........

*An older figure teaching a younger one,*
*who is seated and listening calmly.*

A SMALL AMOUNT of Fire cannot compare to the Sun. When it enters a situation that the Sun already holds, it must not assume that it knows more than everyone else in the room. However, the Sun and Fire are very closely linked, and there is much to learn from the older master.

This is therefore a reading of not wasting the opportunity to learn from someone more capable—recognize their expertise and seek out opportunities to add to your own strength.

The restraint is important, because if the student tries to compete then they will be completely outmatched. This is not Air's intellectual learning, but Fires, and that means that the student is putting their very essence into the task: it is important to them, they are emotionally attached to it in a way that could blow up in anger or frustration. Fire and Sun's interactions are always charged with this bristling potential for heat, so you must instead see the huge opportunity and be grateful for the wise guidance of a good teacher.

Do not doubt yourself though. The Sun's influence here means that you will brush off obstacles and other people's anger. As long as you approach this strange, strained pairing with humility, the Sun's energy will make sure that you come out smiling. The disruptive Fire coming to the Sun ends up as lesser, and the Sun retains the power in the situation. This is a very positive result! It suggests safety, and the defeat of those whose will is opposed to the existing Sun.

If you think that the Fire could be you, and you don't love the current Sun and want to replace it, then you should pause and reflect. The Sun is superior to Fire not just in strength but in purity and sacredness. It knows more, it delivers positive things more safely and frequently than Fire's ragged and shorter flame. True, due to its links to royalty, laws, and power, it is possible for a Sun to become a dictator who should be opposed—but look carefully. Have humility. Even if your situation is about only you in isolation, Lesser Fire over Sun tells you to beware. The Fire is so hopelessly outclassed here, you want to make sure that if you are not the Sun, you do not invoke its wrath.

If you can act with restraint and be humble, the rewards are enormous. Magical work could involve a deity or more powerful being, but it is one that will recognize a kinship between you. You are made of two kinds of the same Fire. Academic studies will have the same relationship—there is a teacher you can learn from, so make sure you do.

The Lesser Fire here is a distraction that will be discarded without even feeling its attack. This is great news if you are absolutely sure that you are the Sun, otherwise ... allow yourself to learn more before you try to test your strength.

# Greater Water over Sun

## The Dream Master

Succeeding at a task of impossible scale;
powerful control of your emotions and imagination

...........

*A standing figure with one hand outstretched,*
*dictating changes to a vast landscape.*

WATER AND FIRE are often in opposition, and the Sun is an invincible fire. Water managing to overcome the sun here is remarkable, but this combination requires the victory to have happened in watery ways. When the subject of such extreme power is the Sun itself, this suggests that the route of success is linked to ideas and hopes that are bigger than the usual small topics of daily life.

In dreams, we can break the rules—no matter how intimidating a thing is, we can change it or overcome it. This requires a lot of control and happens in a place where our fears and inner hopes are visible. This reading therefore has a lot of mystical or dreamlike energy to it, where Water sets the agenda.

There is the danger that the Greater Water can overwhelm you. The Sun is usually a very positive element, and the image of drowning it under an enormous amount of Water, or being completely hidden from sight by a massive storm, can easily be interpreted as a tide of unwanted emotions hiding the warming light. The Sun illuminates the path and reveals hidden dangers for us—so when we go on without its guidance in the very changeable world of Water, we will need to be sure that we can steer without help. If you are in control of the emotions here (and if you can see past Water's illusions), then you will achieve amazing things.

By using dream logic, where size does not link to strength, an ocean of feeling does not have to overwhelm you. You can be outside the effects of it and be its master—still mingling with the Water, still a part of it, but not at the mercy of its effects. By merging with the huge wave you will be able to steer it instead to do the unexpected.

The key to this reading is that the water is coming and the safest thing is to just dive in. Leave the rational, easily-seen world behind, and go with your heart. This is not as totally reckless as it sounds because Water is not the quick, angry energy of Fire: Water contains sympathy, understanding and mystery. It works with intuition instead of blindly reacting or flaring up without planning the way that Fire can.

The Sun has strong connections to science while Water has links to the unconscious and unknown, and even to the Moon. By moving from one to the other you are journeying to a place where your inner thoughts and feelings are absolutely important. Listen to them, and don't assume that a more routine or sensible approach is the best for you. This message is that you should follow your feelings to their maximum extent—swim in them, dream them, and finally master them.

# Lesser Water over Sun

## The Rainbow

Positive emotions, caring and supportive attitude

...........

*A rainbow curving in bright sunlight,*
*from over green fields down into a lake.*

PURELY IN TERMS of strength, this could be seen as throwing a small amount of water at the actual Sun. The Water hisses and is immediately boiled away into vapor, failing to achieve anything. That isn't how this reading ends, though, due to the nature of both of the elements involved...

While it is likely that Water taking any action to assert itself over the Sun will fail, a gentle mix of Water and Sun creates beauty in this oracle. We can see this in the reading for Lesser Sun over Water as well—"Diamonds in the Stream." There, the small amount of sunlight hits a moving river and illuminates the tips of the waves. By contrast in this reading for the Rainbow, it is the water that is barely present and sunlight that is the main component, and moisture in the air modifies the normal beams of light to create a spectrum of colors, which inspires those who see it.

In this way, the Water actually succeeds instead of being cruelly boiled away. The emotions corresponding to water are those that the viewer ends up feeling when they see the rainbow, even when the Water is lesser in strength here. They can be emotions of caring, of adding in a loving way without trying to dominate, or of patiently appreciating beauty. It is important to face up to when you cannot gain your final goal right now, but it is also important not to give up. Water's possible emotion of hopelessness at being lesser is transformed here, into hope and relaxation.

Water has a huge range of positive emotion to draw on, and there is never a bad time to put that into the world. If now isn't the right time for your end goal, then be good to all those involved in the situation until things change, and don't give up. The likelihood of short-term defeat for whichever plan had Water trying to dominate does not mean that you should stop planning, stop hoping, or waiting for a day when your resources are greater. In the meantime, relax and enjoy the sights with a feeling of love and cooperation. When elements combine gently with understanding and grace, new beauty can be created. Despite being a combination with a lesser strength in it, which can often feel like a defeat, this pairing gives hope. Rainbows have in the past been considered a promise from gods—they cause the heart to lift, not to sink. Remember that feeling and hold onto it if you encounter setbacks. They won't be forever, and great things are also on the way.

# Greater Earth over Sun

## The Farmer

A hero hidden by normality, success by mundane means

...........

*A figure planting seeds in a field of turned brown soil.*

THE ANSWER TO the shining promise of the Sun is a large amount of solid, dependable Earth. This may sound unusual, like a mound of soil and rock smothering a bright light, but that is not the case this time. Earth represents (among many other things) regular, dependable work, and it can be a secure and powerful route to success. The Sun is often associated with positive outcomes, but also with a very personal idea of the individual reaching their full potential. The needs that are being met are healthy and important and this combination says that the way to reach them is with more and more Earth.

The Farmer is an often-overlooked figure: they work in a way that requires them to know the Earth in great detail and bring forth life from it. Do not be fooled by the mundane appearance of such a role, many higher magical goals can be gained by throwing yourself strongly into slow and steady practice. It may not seem exciting or prestigious but this is the stuff that quiet heroes are made of.

This pairing tells us not to run after fame and fortune, but instead to concentrate on doing the work. It is a move away from shiny glory to dependable (but maybe less exciting) roots. Other elements such as Moon or Fire can bring in sacred, mysterious, or riskier answers than this, but Earth is centered in very physical real-world sensations.

It also has many links to money (from the metals and precious gems contained in the ground to the ability to grow crops, graze animals and other routes to wealth). Taking time to do the less exciting work will pay off just as well as shooting for the ultimate glory would, and it's more dependable this way.

Remember the Sun's light, and remember why you are working. The big danger with this combination is that you are indeed smothering what could be a beautiful light under tons of Earth. Watch for that. The Earth is necessary, it's going to happen, but don't automatically let it be the entire picture: keep the higher ideals in your mind for later.

A Sun under the Earth is like having a heater under the soil. In winter the memory of the Sun will keep the fields alive and keep cold feet moving. It fights the frosts and gives energy and motivation when we are tiring. So take comfort in Earth's resilience, in its ability to shelter us, neutralize danger and energy, and produce healthy life—but remember the more exciting Sun that you've seen before as well, and plan to eventually bring it back.

In the short term, do the work. If you want to progress, it's going to take honest effort, but it will pay off with all the fruit and harvest you could seek.

# Lesser Earth over Sun

## Discarding the Mask

Recognition for your achievements,
someone liking you for who you are

...........

*A mask pulled away from a face,*
*with blinding light showing behind it.*

The Sun is a glorious, awe-inspiring light, and here the element of Earth is not strong enough to overcome it. Earth (with its heavy rock and enduring strength) is often used to represent the normal things that tie us to our routine: work, the home, solid daily reality. Here, those aspects fail to overcome the beauty of the stronger Sun and it shines out regardless.

Having your light seen by others can be an amazing experience that leads to rewards and recognition. It also means that you can't deny those actions or hide the truth. Behave as though everything will be seen to a greater extent than usual, and you will gain a great deal.

The Sun is also special. The Sun and Moon in this oracle have an aspect of the sacred to them—they are bigger than the elements we can touch, and affect us on more mythic levels. If someone else sees the Sun in you, they don't just see you being good at something: they see the real you that mundane reality fails to hide.

That reality, the strong connection with what you truly think and feel, works both ways. This pairing tells you not to deceive yourself. We all have daily masks that we put on to interact with people so that we don't cause tension. We have one for school or work, another for being around our family without bringing up the old arguments or starting new ones. It is very important that you remember the real you underneath is a much purer, more powerful version than the one that has to walk in the world. We like to think that the Sun doesn't hide, but magically it represents many things that are not physical and not easy for us to be every day. There is a perfection to the golden Sun and a near-infinite power. It has been associated with gods and goddesses for millennia, and we constantly owe our life to its influence on the planet, plants and ourselves. Take the time to reconnect with your best self, with your true motivations and needs. Doing so can be quite a ride, as the Sun is an exhilarating and successful element to embody.

This is a reading about you being seen clearly, and the daily world trying but failing to cover you up again. It's about scrubbing away the dirt to reconnect with your ideals. Others will see the power in your steps if you are following your true path.

It's also a warning to look at what you hide from yourself. We can put up thick walls of rock against painful things or inconvenient feelings: they are blasted into rubble here, because the truth exposed by the Sun's light is too important to who we are to ignore. Check the masks you have put up against the world, but also those you use on yourself. Find the real answer further inside.

# Greater Sun over Sun

## The Triumphant Sun
Unmitigated success; health, vitality, rightness

...........

*A huge yellow sun, with bright burning light all around it.*

The majority of concepts that the Sun symbolizes are very positive: health, truth, success, high energy, the revealing of knowledge. To have this Sun met with another Greater Sun means that this reading is incredibly full of energy. It's as though a summer Sun was then reinforced with another larger one.

This will blast through just about any obstacle. Nothing gets in the way. This unfortunately includes you, so make sure that you're ready for this much energy. There is going to be a lot of light shone upon all places, which could lead to the discovery of secrets.

The dangers are clear: unrestrained Sun can lead to drought and create desert. It has also stood for male power, or a strict ruler, so you should watch to make sure you are not caught in another's power. Ride the pouring of energy from this Sun yourself, and the day will be bright and golden.

If you are wondering whether you will succeed at something when you receive this reading, the answer is "YES!" This is the entry in this oracle that contains the highest amount of success. If events feel blocked or crooked at the moment, the Sun's energy will clear the way for smooth and healthy progress.

This is also a confirmation that you are currently doing the right thing. Sun moving to Sun means that it was successful last time, and it will be successful again. Keep doing the thing.

When we work with the Sun in magic there is very little room for self-doubt or anxiety. The golden light simply burns away the darker places where those feelings could hide and gives us a strong, constant confidence in our chest. It reveals truth and dispels darkness. This forceful light is simple when we work alone, but it can be unbalancing when other elements are paired with it. Thankfully there is nothing here to stop the reach of its rays, nothing to seek to change its energy or replace it. There is only more glorious Sun, free to act according to its nature.

And that nature is frequently glorious. This double Sun can make us look at the best parts of ourselves—those that cause us to feel worthy, honorable, and happy. Elsewhere in the oracle the pairing of Greater Sun over Fire is titled "The Knighthood." It includes the idea that becoming a knight is not something that changes you but recognition of the qualities you have already been demonstrating. This is even more true for Greater Sun over Sun. This is not a meeting of a master and junior, but a movement from a beginning place that had already reached mastery.

There are aspects to explore in all this blinding light, but the overall lesson is simple: enormous success.

# Lesser Sun over Sun

Small corrections to an already successful
course; good use of restraint and timing

...........

*A large yellow Sun with a smaller
one overlapping it on the lower left.*

INSTEAD OF TRYING to dominate, the new influence coming in here is a supportive Lesser Sun, which lends its skill and clear vision of the truth to an existing endeavor. One hazard often associated with Sun is arrogance, or forcing authority onto others. Here, the new Sun knows better and deliberately stands behind, helping only as much as is wanted. With this careful restraint, they can make further refinements to an existing plan.

This can be a warning as well—take your time, don't try to directly challenge. It could be worth submitting to someone else's authority if it means that you will be influential behind the scenes or taken on as part of a loyal team. The best route here is one of subtlety and fine detail … which is ironic because fine detail is exactly what this reading hides from us. It takes some Sun and adds more Sun in a way that suggests failure. The reason is that there's simply too much of the same kind of light, and no shadows to give it texture.

The historical associations of the Sun suggest that it's very focused in just one direction, always striving to achieve and valuing success. It's an extrovert, being seen by others and recognized for its brilliance. What this reading completely lacks is any other color of light. The Lesser Sun has been rejected, it is not the answer, so we can deduce that a change needs to happen—a new influence needs to be brought in.

The Sun is conventional and acceptable. It contains many great properties and is extremely positive, but it only does one thing. This combination often signals that we should spend some time with Water or the Moon as well, something that is less fixed in its direction. A path that breaks the rules a little bit, or provides us with time in the cool shade.

This reading says that endlessly pursuing success is not enough color for life. "Success" is overrated when there are new experiences to pursue in all areas: new things to learn, fun actions to take, emotions to explore, security to relax in, dark sanctuaries to find self-reflection. When the Sun is at noon all the time, there are no shadows to be seen. Everything becomes washed-out and blinding. To navigate your way through that requires knowledge of more ways to be than just Sun.

The influence of the Sun means that despite all these warnings, no matter how this applies the situation will be a happy and positive one. It just contains a message that the time is coming to try something else as well. Use skill and intelligence to steer through the change ahead, and the Sun's excellent properties will mean that wherever your path leads it will continue to deliver good things.

# Greater Moon over Sun

## The Eclipse

A powerfully magical feeling; mystery triumphs

..........

*A silver Moon ringed by a golden Sun, surrounded by stars.*

THE SUN IS sure of itself, constant in its strength and power. The Moon is more chaotic, always changing, leaving shadows and then going entirely dark. The Sun's light shines powerfully into every hidden corner and reveals what is there, linking it to science and truth, while the Moon's light gives an eerie glow to nighttime paths and activities, creating many links to folklore and magic.

Here though, the Moon has overcome the Sun. Its white light is beautiful, emotional, and peaceful. It shows that the existence of a lesser-known partner will be seen over the more famous one. It suggests that magic will triumph over science.

Be sure not to take this too far—these two elements are not enemies, and the Sun is still supportive even if it is no longer the largest influence. (It is, after all, the Sun's light that reflects from the surface of the Moon.) There is no need to choose only one completely. Nevertheless, this is a rare success and should be celebrated: it is a move away from the rational and into a perhaps more beautiful world where feelings and dreams rule instead.

In most readings, this pairing signifies a big and deliberate change. The situation was the Sun, and soon it will be a Greater Moon. These things are not remotely the same, and you need to acknowledge that. If you have been going through days of normality, focusing on how you are seen by others and working at keeping everything happy, then it is time to let go of that breath and spend time with the Moon.

The Moon's magic is of course nocturnal. It works during the quiet nights, with darkness as a blanket. It has no use for logic, science or obvious "cause and effect," proceeding instead along invisible connections and willpower. It reminds us of our primal nature and breaks the rules of society. Gifts of the Moon include the chance to be yourself outside of society's expectations, the ability to look inside for answers without being told how they should be reached, and the chance to commune with a sacred power.

This means that in any area of life—even something as predictable as daily work—the action that is recommended is to look within. Use psychic skills, work with dreams and magic to find different answers. Take time for your private self instead of the mask that you show the world.

A final point to consider is that the Moon overcoming the Sun is an eclipse. This is a total inversion of normality, an upset of time (night in the middle of the day), and a triumph of magic and spirituality over the usual calendar. If you are asking the oracle about a specific event, this can signal an unexpected reversal or opposite outcome.

Trust your intuition and make time for the more personal aspects of life that you might have been leaving out. Look inside yourself for answers, only relying on those who can share that dark sacred space with you. There may be opportunities to escape to an unexpected place away from the gaze of others or to turn a situation absolutely upside down.

# Lesser Moon over Sun

Reflecting in another's glory; invisibility,
ability to hide from unwanted attention

...........

*A large Sun, with a smaller moon almost unseen to its left.*
*The Moon is an empty circle with no color of its own.*

MOONLIGHT IS ALWAYS made from reflected sunlight. In this reading, the Moon isn't trying to compete—its own reflected glow is so small compared to the Sun that it is all but invisible.

There are many advantages to being unseen. It can also be useful to deliberately allow yourself to be a small mirror for another's light. Sometimes this is because the other person has more experience and it would be dangerous to challenge them, or the pressures that come with being in the spotlight are not worth the reward.

It's true that you can be ignored if there is a brighter light nearby, and it's also true that concentrating on the reflection itself can lead to too much vanity or introspection. Instead, realize that this is a relaxing, stable place to be, and use this privacy to achieve your goals. A big distraction can be great for allowing you to keep your secrets.

Remember though that the Moon has failed here and is of lesser strength. The Sun still rules, and the golden light could reveal truth … so make sure you don't mind those secrets getting out or be ready with a story about them. The Moon hides activities or creates darker shadows around them, while the Sun works to expose them. This mirror made of a Moon is therefore an odd one.

Hiding in plain sight and hoping people look away from you is a risky plan. The invisibility mentioned so far is not certain, so it can be safer to be the Sun, to throw yourself into the publicly-seen actions that will gain you approval even if you'd rather be alone or making more personal time. It's not always enough to rely on the reflection from others if you need a place to hide in or to exist in— if you put the work in yourself and aim to be the Sun, then other pretenders who try to steal your spotlight will not succeed.

The Lesser Moon next to the shining Sun is very hard to detect due to the blinding object nearby. It can symbolize something that is clearly there but easily missed unless you look harder than usual. If you can find that object then the information you gain will be valuable and related to your inner self.

Unlike some readings in this oracle (which are about just one issue transforming into another, or the emotional state created by two elements), this one is focused on the relationship between two very separate influences and their relative visibility. The mirror shows us some harsh truths. It can mean that we have been stealing the spotlight, or not appreciating friends who let us take the glory. In all the many permutations, since the Moon is lesser it will be safer to take action to ensure you are the Sun. If you're sure you want to use a misty mirror to hide in, be aware that it is a risk.

# Greater Air over Moon

## THE SCIENTIST
Far-ranging ideas, new and innovative
thinking outside boundaries

...........

*A figure in a white lab coat, working excitedly in a book.*

THE CORRESPONDENCES FOR Moon and Air are not very similar. Moon has more in common with Water, leading to dreams, emotions, and a sense of the intangible. Air on the other hand is linked to hard logic, communication of ideas, and sharp thought. When it comes in and replaces the existing Moon in a reading, it is a move away from mysteries and toward planning and academic insight.

The Moon retains some influence, meaning that the quick thinking here will be in areas outside of the normal ones. They may be a project that is a secret obsession or lead someone to abandon the usual paths for a new intuitive route.

Either way, there is a marked increase in order and effectiveness. Air's clear sight and lack of blockages mean that progress will be quick. Vague outlines are made sharp by the use of logic and knowledge.

This is usually a positive change. We all want help with mysteries and dark, shifting situations. Greater Air is an absolutely brilliant solution for that, giving us the whole picture in a way we can clearly see it in our minds. It's a promise that all will become clear and that mental planning is the way forward.

While it is useful for finding answers and winning quizzes, replacing the Moon with Greater Air does mean that you lose out on all the things that the Moon can offer. These include a certain softness, a forgiving environment to explore in, and the connection to our intuition. These will be less available here as the energy moves toward conscious thought instead.

The best way to take advantage of this shift is to make lists. Test your assumptions. Talk to others about it, and think about their points of view as well. Get clever with your question and think about it again and again, because the time for an instant intuitive guess is over. (This is the only reading that essentially says "Stop using this oracle and—instead of exploring your intuition—try just writing down your thoughts clearly.")

This pairing shows an increase in focus and gives us the ability to see things as they truly are without illusion. That's a valuable gift in a world pulled by Water's needs, Fire's wants, and Earth's inertia. Use Air's freedom and clarity to think your way calmly around the issue and make sure you capture all the sides of it: don't be swayed by emotion, especially the private yearning or shifting of the Moon.

# Lesser Air over Moon

## THE EXPLORER

Ongoing mystery, a refusal to give up secrets

...........

*A patient figure standing still, regarding the Moon.*

THE MOON'S PULL calls to our blood, our dreams, and our imagination. It can often feel that it would be safer to explore these things with a little detachment and organization—the kind that Air brings. That has been rejected here, though.

This is an excellent combination for exploring your dreams or inner hopes, and it can lead to important new adventures. The Moon governs strong needs and emotions. It promises new changes and exists outside of the normal rules. While staying true to the spirit of the unknown country that the Moon represents, the Explorer can journey on in a profound way.

Doing so in a manner that is compatible with the Moon is the important point. Don't try to approach this rationally; that has been tried and discarded as lesser. There's still a hint of it around, enough to let you plan and act, but this journey is going to be a fully magical exercise that relies more on instinct than thought. Any attempt to analyze the situation using only book-learning or academic study will fail. The Moon's mystery will not be reduced now, and any religious or spiritual feeling that you have will not be put aside: investigate the Moon's energy seriously and don't try to retreat behind the daily world's dry logic.

If you were asking the oracle about a situation at home or work, then this answer means you need to go with your heart instead of trying to use rational arguments. The best speeches and clearly true facts won't be effective here, it needs a more primal approach. The Moon is connected to Water and the tides, to darkness and shape-changing. If you have a decision to make, that is where you must go. If someone else needs to be convinced on an issue, speaking the total truth from your innermost place is the key. Don't try to be clever, be pure. Spend time alone listening to your inner voice, or use some of the rituals included in this book to help you receive magical information more easily.

Air might have failed here as the main answer, but its presence in small amounts still makes everything easier. Air brings space and freedom, and that works well when the magic we are doing includes the hidden mysteries of the Moon. Space to breathe is space to relax in, to use for security so that we can concentrate on the task in front of us.

This reading suggests that there is more work to do before an answer will come, and that it involves exploring the tricky and moving realms of the Moon. A meditation or deliberate magical ritual for more information is recommended. Know that there is no easy answer, and that the element that was chosen is one that cycles through phases and darkness. This movement and mystery was in place before and remains in place after Air's approach, so the situation is still the murky and changing one it was. The answers will not be easy, and the route to them requires some inner work.

# Greater Fire over Moon

## THE SHOUT

Imposing your will; gathering
your determination and acting strongly

...........

*A wave of Fire rolling over the Moon,*
*with a voice of defiance ringing out.*

THE MOON IS not an entirely safe influence. It holds the potential for unpredictable change and emotional turmoil. With that as the background, Greater Fire coming in becomes a very strong and loud event. It burns away the murky unknowns, imposing Fire's sure belief in itself and confident action.

The Moon often represents the inner emotions we feel in religious experiences or awe at nature. A shout when in this mindset can be extremely powerful. There is no Earth here to provide a grounding influence, no Air for a calmly focused mind; instead, this experience begins in a place of unknown change and rises up with the maximum roaring energy.

Overriding subtle influences with a shout does of course mean that you miss the small details. This doesn't matter, because aligning the Moon to Fire in this way relates it to inner needs that would be useless to ignore anyway. You have to take this route, and defend it, so worrying about the detail isn't the point. This shout comes from your very center, and it is ecstatic.

If you are coming to the oracle without a specific question in mind, then this means an end to mystery and a new leap forward in an exciting direction. Change is going to happen, and what that change is will be revealed soon.

This reading sometimes signifies effective protest or defiance, or passionate opinions that are contrary to the traditional worldview. It tells you that your beliefs are right and that you can follow them if you commit with passion.

Fire includes the issues that we would defend most strongly and loudly, ones that we really believe in. The Moon speaks right to the innermost part of us, to our secret beliefs and needs. When one becomes the other, we are guaranteed to be interested and pleased in the topic that arises. Every time that Greater Fire appears, it answers the question of "Will this change?" with a big "Yes." That's just for physical-world questions; when an issue is magical, this is even stronger. Fire is very effective in areas where we have to use our willpower, and that certainly includes magic.

If there was any advice to give, it is to remember that not everything needs to be shouted. There is a place in the world for subtlety as well, and when you're caught up in strongly using your willpower, you can easily forget the fine details. That isn't too important, since the opportunity to follow your strongly-held beliefs is enriching and life-affirming. You should do it, after the briefest of safety checks.

Be brave, bold, and know that what you feel is right. If you have a Fire in your chest, shout it out. If you don't, find one. We all need conviction, ideals, and causes that we would fight for. They can be people, freedoms, or any number of rights, but you should feel one in your blood and in your bones. When you have that, don't hesitate to shout it.

# Lesser Fire over Moon

## The Mantra

A light to guide the way toward mysteries, repetition

...........

*A Full Moon circled by a thin band of red flame.*

THE MOON IS an odd choice for achieving things in the real world. It hides in shadow, changes its mind, and then comes out blazing and mighty. Fire, by contrast, makes action happen. It moves and burns, giving speed, power, energy, and passion.

When it adds to the mysterious and hidden aspects of the Moon, in a strength that shows the Fire is not trying to dominate, then the energy and movement will help us to explore those shifting secrets. The Fire will light the way in a slower but reliable manner.

For spiritual matters, this is like a mantra: a repeating, passionate but focused action that lifts the heart and moves the blood. It will not be denied, and it will help you to find new answers from its burning need.

You will not have access to the stronger levels of Fire's conviction or fearlessness, but use the smaller amount wisely and you will discover personal truths. If something is challenging you and refuses to make itself totally known, keep the Fire burning. The light will return in a cycle and your determination will still be there. If a situation is frightening, take heart from the Fire inside you. Remind yourself of what you want, and concentrate on having courage to make action happen.

Repetition is key here. Both the Moon and Fire are connected to the issues we feel strongly about at the most personal level.

Unlike a Greater Fire, however, this is not the time to be totally certain of the rightness of your decision. This is a very quiet reading. The Moon hangs in silent solitude and the Fire stays as embers. Fire's noisier aspects (of fast action and aggression) are absent.

Since the Lesser Fire shows that Fire's approach was not the way, we should look again to Moon for guidance on how to proceed. The Moon challenges us to ask questions, to seek answers in the darkness instead of the dependable endurance of Earth or emotional flow of Water. While it's clear that we shouldn't disrupt the Moon's silent beauty with too much Fire, there is still some of that lesser element involved here. That tells us not to give up on the thing we know is right, but to keep it burning. This is a reading of the Moon, but the constant low red glow of Fire will keep us on the road we want.

That can be difficult under the Moon's shifting shadows. This is where the repetition comes in: if you are thrown off the path, get back on it. If you doubt yourself or are afraid by the terrors in the night, tell yourself again and again that you know the way. The Fire is a determination in your gut, a fuel for your motivation. It says that you will not give up and will not change course. It is a light in your hand when the darkness is frightening.

But keep that Fire low. No one knows it all, and this pairing says that an obvious and loud Fire is not the direction to go in. Keep looking inside for better answers and don't assume that you see the whole story yet. The Moon and only a Lesser Fire do not provide enough light for you to be absolutely certain of the right way to travel, so bide your time and keep your eyes open. Take heart, stay strong, and hold onto your beliefs as events cycle past.

# Greater Water over Moon

## TREASURE IN THE DEPTHS
Yearning for something out of reach, powerlessness

...........

*The Moon as a gigantic white*
*pearl glowing under the weight of an ocean.*

THE MOON OFFERS us dreams and otherworldly perfection, but here it has been buried under a greater amount of Water. While these two are connected, the Moon is the more sacred and elevated of the two—to have it overcome by mundane Water is to be robbed of the purer version. Emotions are overwhelming here, often signifying grief over a lover you cannot be with or the distracting turmoil that keeps you from the meditative calm you would need to see the Moon more clearly.

The dominant feeling from this combination is one of yearning, being able to see the prize but not reach it. Do not be fooled by the Water that surrounds you—it is less than the prize you could be trying for. Work through it, dive into it, and find the more sacred treasure.

If you swim down, the white glow from the Moon will be seen even if you cannot touch it yet. Do not be distracted. If a sea of emotion is your actual goal, remember that a higher purpose should be at the end of it. And most of all remember that intense emotions will pass, and self-knowledge leads to better outcomes in the future.

There is a tricky balance to be maintained in this reading. The Moon's sacred energy means that we should respect it and strive for it compared to the more mundane Water, but it has been defeated by Greater Water here. This says that our emotions—connections to people, friendship, healing, and peace—are what we need to focus on for the future. The answer lies in a mix of both.

What does a move away from the Moon and toward Water look like? In a way it is similar to the difference between the Sun and Fire: a move away from higher ideals and toward manifestation in the real world, to how it affects our daily lives in the short term instead of how it pulls at our purer selves. While being swamped by a tide of unwanted emotion is never good, here we need to find ways to value Water for its own sake and seek it out in moderation, without forgetting the shining prize that also exists elsewhere.

Primarily this means a journey away from a beautiful but lonely single light and toward an ocean that flows between us and many other people. Water is forgiving and adaptable, it purifies and attracts. It gives us compassion for others, connecting us to the world. There are a lot of good reasons to do this, but it's scary—one of Water's magical maxims is "To Dare."

And there is a reason for that, because there is a stark warning in this pairing as well. When diving into emotion, you don't get to choose which you keep. Water has a darker side, full of jealousy and deceit: it can trick us with illusion and lies, made especially potent because we feel them emotionally. So the message is "Get out there and connect with people, stop having dreams on your own," but don't go too far. Keep the Moon's light in your mind instead of being distracted by the strong tides you swim in.

# Lesser Water over Moon

## The Silvered Dish

Simplicity, silence, divination; calm action to see the truth

...........

*A round silver plate with a small lip, containing some*
*pure water. It glows brightly in the light from the Moon.*

THIS IS ONE of the most mysterious and subtle combinations. The Moon represents inner needs, religious feeling, and incredible quiet beauty. Water is associated with many emotions, as well as the soft empathy that allows us to merge with others and bring their experiences into our own. These two together are very effective. The Moon pulls at the oceans, the tides answer its call. It changes character in the same way that Water does, rising and falling in strength.

When these two meet and the focus is on the Moon, big things happen. In a different combination, The Greater Moon over Water can be a full moon over a roaring, stormy sea. With Lesser Water over Moon, the effect is just the opposite: a serene Moon with its daughter Water acting in a supportive and complimentary way.

The mixture of inner truths and emotions make this an excellent reading for divination or self-reflection. It is a mirror, but made of still water and magic. There will be serene silence and a safe place to meditate. The Moon calls, and the Water will answer, if you dare enough to keep looking.

As always with a lesser strength, keep Water's presence in your mind but don't give in to it in relation to the strength of the Moon here. Water connects us to people but the Moon works on a higher level. It doesn't care about our relationship or the push and pull of daily emotion that we go through. It has purer ideals to follow, and greater mysteries.

It's therefore important to be focused on looking at the light of the Moon, not down at the waves.

There is no roaring Fire here or enquiring Air, it is an extremely relaxed and flowing scene of soft moonlight reflected on the sea. The Water is used to give just enough depth to help us access the Moon's call. That white light above can be understood if we can move away from the depths of the ocean we usually swim in. The Moon has known all the pain and yearning that humankind have thrown toward it for millennia, looking up in the night sky and wishing for their secret desires. It comforts and forgives, then vanishes and slowly returns. We could all use some of that tranquillity and focus when we feel the waves crashing around us.

This is a reading that empowers divination. It also says that Water was not the correct element to overcome the Moon's mysteries and that another might be more successful. Use a mirror to look closely at your real self and choose a new approach that is less caught up in Water's feelings.

# Greater Earth over Moon

## THE FAMILY MEAL
Grounding, returning to mundanity,
recovering from instability

···········

*A group of people eating a meal in a
cozy room. There are no windows to the outside.*

THE MOON AND Earth share a lot in common in the physical world, but their historical correspondences couldn't be much more different. The Moon is elusive, changing, full of shadows, and also beautiful but unreachable light. The Earth is solid, enduring, easy to touch, and capable of taking energy into the ground to disperse it away.

When they meet like this and Earth is greater, it replaces the unpredictable mysteries of the Moon with reliable foundations of rock and soil. The gifts of Earth (food, shelter, a home) all meet to bring down the level of chaos of outside and give us a safe, known environment instead.

Uncertainty or yearning for things that have not yet been grasped can be set aside for a time, and the physical comforts should be enjoyed. Eat heavy food and take care of your body and your emotional needs. We can only manage change in the world if we also have a grounded center to return to.

There are three aspects of Earth that are particularly important to focus on here: one is the home and family. The Moon is alone, but humans cannot afford to be. If you are trying for the Moon and are told Greater Earth instead, you are being told to stop chasing lonely dreams.

Dreams are the second point. Earth gives us sleep in a solid, secure bed. It gives us strong walls and recovery for the physical body. Moon on the other hand gives us unpredictable trickery, constant movement and change of shape, and the leaping between invisible links that is magic. Well, a good sleep secured by Earth is also powerful magic. Looking after your sleep will dramatically improve your life almost immediately.

And the third point is food and nature. It's very easy in modern living to become lost in our heads, assuming that whichever mood or problem we're thinking about is insurmountable and huge. The element of Earth provides food for our bodies and greenery and life for our minds. Both of these can help—if you can't see an answer clearly because your mind is too crowded, then eat something and change your location. We need to be reminded that our feet walk the planet, that our bones are weighed to the ground at all times.

When ritualists do magic, they often perform a "grounding" exercise afterward. This brings you back from any altered or heightened states of consciousness, from sensitive senses or journeys in the mind. It puts your feet firmly back on solid ground and brings your mind back to your body. That kind of grounding is what is needed with this combination too.

This reading is not subtle. It says "Get your head out of the night clouds and spend time on the things that make you secure in your daily life." If your question was a choice between two options, the answer is the one that brings more security (whether that's through dependable money, home comforts, or a stable emotional state). Don't look to wild emotion or furious thinking for the answer here, what is coming is stability. Try it. If it doesn't work and you want to go back to gazing at the Moon, you can do that from a secure footing.

# Lesser Earth over Moon

A gentle return to solid ground
amidst chaos; a lingering feeling of oddness

...........

*A person walking over a white, glowing land,*
*with their feet not touching the ground.*

THE ELEMENT OF Earth has been used to symbolize one mystical action more than any other over the centuries: safely taking away energy. It is used to turn all kinds of unpredictable or harmful influence into a nonmoving, safe state, like a lightning rod that pulls electricity into the ground and away.

There can be a good reason to do this when working with the Moon, because there are no hard edges in that work. The Moon's misty glow is a strange and luminous light unlike anything we're used to during the day. Its mysteries involve cycles, shadows, and the cover of night. It's all too easy to feel disconnected from reality if we spend too long working in that higher realm without reminding ourselves of the solid daily life we also have on Earth.

And that's exactly what has happened here. The comforting, supportive energy of Earth was not enough to overcome the Moon's call. Those seeking solid ground won't find it yet.

There are a lot of good reasons to stay up in the night sky. If you want to explore a mysterious place full of inner meaning, and to find something that matters to you on a serious emotional level, it is a place rich with answers. Exploring dreams and sacred feelings are always worthwhile, and going down the rabbit hole can give you answers you can't gain anywhere else.

This does mean that the potential for getting lost in illusion or unreality is high. It's as if you're a balloon and the string tying you to Earth just broke. (If you're thinking that sounds like a fun plan with no drawbacks, then that may be the problem.)

How this translates into answering the typical questions we have about daily life is complex. If you have a choice between the sensible option and something that your heart yearns for, this reading rejects the Earth connection and gives you permission to chase the dreams. It also implies that there is no security coming—that you'll need to feel rooted in your normal routine by yourself, because the future will be really odd.

This doesn't have to be a problem. The Moon winning over Earth is a rejection of normality, a move into an extended time of psychic awareness and information coming to you on a level that is unusual. Secrets and intuition are particularly active. If mundane life has been stopping something feeling magical to you, then that magic won't be blocked for much longer.

Earth is also linked to money (not just as metal in the ground, but to provide for worldly comforts and secure the home). This pairing can therefore mean that the goal you're chasing might not have the money to back it up in the short term—if that's a problem, concentrate on bringing in more Earth.

The Moon's strength here suggests that dreams and hopes could make themselves felt, but more work needs to be done to bring them into the real world. Provided that chasing dreams and finding fulfilling answers was your goal, this is great news. If you just wanted a normal day instead then you're going to need to concentrate on keeping things sensible—because events could send them a little wild.

# Greater Sun over Moon

## The Queen Crowned

Success in magic, control and
skill over inner work, personal success

...........

*A Full Moon in the bottom of the image,
with a blazing Sun hanging above it.*

THE SUN AND Moon are not always included in a list of classical elements. When they appear in this oracle, they draw on centuries of symbolism and correspondences (as well as being holy and powerful lights with links to the other elements of Fire and Water).

This means that a reading featuring both the Sun and the Moon is packed with magical or sacred energy. This particular combination began with Moon as its basis, and the Sun came in strength to meet its challenge and succeed. The Sun's own magic is a much more visible and knowable sort than that of the Moon. The golden light has been connected to science, revealing truth in exactly the dark corners that the waxing and waning Moon creates. While this can still be answering magic with magic, the Sun's route is usually of mastering something with glorious skill.

Two heavenly bodies of light battling it out above us is an amazing show, and the forces involved are on a scale we do not usually reach. The person who succeeds as the Sun here shows great knowledge and authority, with a burning golden energy pushing it onwards to destiny.

This is the reading that depicts the solving of important mysteries, and understanding where there was previously delusion or lack of sight. It definitely isn't about normal matters—relationships, security, or chance events. This is a revelation on an internal level.

It's also the story of a journey, from Moon's non-material dreams to the Sun's easily seen achievement. The Moon was in this situation first and prepared the way for the Sun to triumph. The Moon is therefore a road you could take if you want to eventually get to the Sun's success. Some paths are solved by steady work, some by passion or clever speech. This one is found by silently looking inward and aiming for greater things, then taking that action outwards. Don't let the usual concerns about what is reasonable stop you. Don't tell yourself no before you start. Both the elements here are at a distance away from our planet, only reaching out to us with their rays—you won't gain either of them by using solutions we can find at ground level.

That fact that Sun is greater here does mean that you should be open and visible in what you think and do. Moon's hidden thoughts can start you on the road, but to see the end you must let others feel the heat and see the light of your success. Don't hide, and don't work on anything that you're not ready for other people to see.

# Lesser Sun over Moon

## The Attentive Spouse
A reliable partner, supportive or
correct behavior, a productive team
···········
*Two people, one engaged in work while the
other stands back and considerately lends their energy.*

The Sun is powerful enough to make the Moon invisible, but here it chooses not to. The Sun can often take glory in a selfish way but this is instead about teamwork. Sun and Moon together are a mix of beautiful energies, and when they stop trying to compete, then the image is one of uncomplicated joy.

There is also a tremendous amount of power. Even with the Sun showing restraint, neither of these are normal elements. Everything they do is on a level above, as strong as the Sun is to a normal Fire that humans could make with wood. When these two celestial powers act in harmony, nothing can stop them.

This reading shows cooperation in a process, but it doesn't have to mean two different people. It could be visualized as the larger Sun voluntarily dimming, and the smaller Moon being given enough light to compete, so that both of them become regarded as the same strength and can work together. The image can therefore be of one situation with two wheels turning smoothly to everyone's benefit.

It's also a warning. A Lesser Sun with any element can often mean that success won't happen. Here it says that instead of rushing forward to full success, you need to look at the quieter partner and pay attention to their needs. They hold the power to stop your progress, so only both of you working together will move it forward—if you try to go alone, the Moon will outshine the Sun. The Moon holds the power here.

Make sure that your reasons for teaming up are good ones. Don't try to win by copying others instead of being your genuine self, and don't settle for reflected fame. This is a deliberate partnership that benefits both parties. Both should compromise and agree to hold part of themselves back in order to better serve the partnership. If you do this, then the end result will be more than you could accomplish alone.

This is especially true if you are usually the one with the most power. This is a humbling reading, of those who usually stride to expected success being stopped by a power that was expected to be smaller. Look carefully at small or hidden details of your situation, or your innermost instincts. If what you're doing is conflicting with your dreams for the future, you could be holding yourself back.

At a simple level, this combination tells us to find a friend and get some help (or look forward to being helped, even if that is unexpected).

# Greater Moon over Moon

## THE FULL MOON
Magical power, night, religion;
absolute success of spiritual work

...........

*A Full Moon in the upper-center of the image, with the top*
*half of another Moon rising up from the bottom edge.*

THE MOON REPRESENTS magic, sacredness, and mystery. It is
not concerned with food in your stomach, warm rooms with
strong walls, or physical comforts. It stands beautiful but distant,
moving through phases in a dance, inspiring humanity with its
glow. When that is the only influence in a reading, the energy
is extremely disconnected from physical needs. It is focused on
disembodied dreams and mental journeys. It rises to realms of
silver light in the dark.

This is a strong but difficult reading. It represents big changes
in your inner world and an absolute rejection of normality. It begins with Moon and follows with—instead of all the other influences that could have diluted it—maximum Moon. Outside
energies are blown aside by the power of a Full Moon in the
night. Any goals involving dreams, magic, or spirituality will succeed strongly. Any matters of a more earthly nature do not get
attention while this happens.

There are great opportunities here … but they are only on subjects that interest the Moon, and nothing else. These can be secrets that you hide from others or inner changes that you must
go through.

When casting an oracle for the day ahead, if you receive this reading (particularly with a six for the greater strength, showing all sixes), then you know you are in for a ride. This is a massive shot of wild lunar energy with no balance to it at all.

It can be difficult to interpret this combination. It doesn't relate easily to the common questions we ask: on love, or money, or how to solve problems. It's often a religious or magical reading, one that says we will find important new truths for our inner life. That's not always convenient when we have a nine-to-five job that day.

Be open to new experiences when this combination appears. Pay attention to how powerful you feel, and make time for inner work even at the expense of more mundane tasks. The Full Moon at its greatest strength has a wild energy that is linked with madness—you can expect things to get a little weird.

There is a lot to be grateful for with this combination as well. If you are someone who uses divination then you already have interests that are not typical. The Moon dominating like this represents the success of all alternative thought over the rational aspects of Earth, Sun, or Air, which sometimes oppose it. It is a triumph of magic over logic, of mystical awe in the night. It's a very strong answer. If it doesn't seem to fit your question, then look very hard at what it could be saying instead, because at this strength the message will be important.

# Lesser Moon over Moon

## THE PHASES OF THE MOON
Flexibility and adaptability, constant slow change

..........

*A series of moons from left to right*
*at different phases of fullness. Complete dark*
*through thin crescents to full circle, and then back.*

THE CHANGING VISIBLE shape of the Moon has always affected humanity's emotions when we look at it. It does not give full light all the time, but cycles through half strength and into darkness. Historically it has even been linked to deities of thieves and those who want to be hidden, because the half-light allows these activities to be possible.

The cycle of changes, of white and black, can be a comfort. Resting is as important as movement. This reading is about that movement and how one obvious answer is not always the best route to take.

There is a lot here that is unknown: the Moon is dancing to its own tune, leaving and returning over weeks (where the Sun would have stayed constant). As well as getting caught up in illusion or deception in these shifting shadows, this pairing can foretell someone who changes their mind without warning or whose motives you don't understand.

It is not a high-energy reading, though. The light leaves and returns. The Moon travels at its own pace. There is a lot of potential for you to find a comfortable place within that journey, as long as you remember to be adaptable. When it comes to interpreting this for real-world events, it says that there is definitely not a fixed final time when something will happen—it is likely to continue instead.

This is a very reflective reading. If we take the view that change is inevitable, then we soon start seeing things in the longer-term. If events will always change, then there is no need to worry about each of those small changes. In time it will change back anyway.

And if you want some change to happen instead of things staying the same, there is hope for that within this combination too. There is light and dark, and room for everyone to find what they need between the total absence and the brightest light.

The correspondences of the Moon draw us away from earthly concerns and toward romance and primal thoughts. Having the situation begin with the Moon and then have a Lesser Moon enter the picture says that "more Moon" was not the answer. We need to remember the vibrant colors, smells, and mess of the rest of life as well. Part of the lesson of the phases of the Moon is that there are times when the Moon itself is not the focus—it appears absent, or dark, and we should remember that other parts of life should also have these changes in them. Seek out the other elements for the best route to take, because solely focusing on one thing just isn't how healthy lives work. (This can lead to casting a second oracle and paying close attention to non-Moon elements within it!)

11

# Afterword

DURING THE WRITING of this book I realized that I have been using, refining, and teaching the dice oracle for over ten years. It has connected people more closely to the vibrant, life-giving elements in the world around them and opened a window into the shifting patterns of fate. Now that it will reach an even wider audience, I have only one piece of advice left to give: start a journal.

It can be a good idea to keep a journal of your results when working with any divination system, and certainly with this oracle. Not only will this show you which readings you received over time, but it can also help to record your own interpretations of the pairings. The notes on the previous pages are not the final answer—the reading is "Greater/Lesser X over Y," and the final conclusion that you come to from there can be entirely from your own feelings on each combination. As you work further with the elements, you might find that you prefer the meeting of physical Fire and Water more than using their magical correspondences, or a mix of both. This is all valuable information to keep in a journal.

Using dice for divination in combination with books is a practice that goes back millennia. I hope that the oracle will bring you wisdom and joy while lighting the path ahead for your own journey with the elements.

# Appendix

| Dice Roll | Elements | Title | Summary | Page |
|---|---|---|---|---|
| 1, 1, 1–3 | Lesser Air over Air | The Advisor | Subtle and wise advice | 60 |
| 1, 1, 4–6 | Greater Air over Air | The Free Skies | Freedom; the chance to soar | 58 |
| 1, 2, 1–3 | Lesser Air over Fire | The Bellows | Measured control, creation according to plan | 84 |

| Dice Roll | Elements | Title | Summary | Page |
|-----------|----------|-------|---------|------|
| 1, 2, 4–6 | Greater Air over Fire | Conflagration | Explosive increase, massive energy for success | 82 |
| 1, 3, 1–3 | Lesser Air over Water | The Tranquil Lake | Peace, calm, leisure; safety to ride with the current | 108 |
| 1, 3, 4–6 | Greater Air over Water | The Confidant | Sensible advice, a person who is outside of the emotional upset | 106 |
| 1, 4, 1–3 | Lesser Air over Earth | Seeds Borne on the Wind | Successful fertility, nature working to aid all things | 132 |

| Dice Roll | Elements | Title | Summary | Page |
|-----------|----------|-------|---------|------|
| 1, 4, 4–6 | Greater Air over Earth | The Shaking House | Bringing freedom to a stagnant situation | 130 |
| 1, 5, 1–3 | Lesser Air over Sun | The Spring Morning | Good conditions for relaxed contemplation | 156 |
| 1, 5, 4–6 | Greater Air over Sun | The Governess | Good guidance, steering the currents to find the best answer | 154 |
| 1, 6, 1–3 | Lesser Air over Moon | The Explorer | Ongoing mystery, a refusal to give up secrets | 180 |
| 1, 6, 4–6 | Greater Air over Moon | The Scientist | Far-ranging ideas, new and innovative thinking | 178 |

| Dice Roll | Elements | Title | Summary | Page |
|---|---|---|---|---|
| 2, 1, 1–3 | Lesser Fire over Air | The Snuffed Candle | Controlling emotion cleverly | 64 |
| 2, 1, 4–6 | Greater Fire over Air | Passion | Joy, heart overruling the head | 62 |
| 2, 2, 1–3 | Lesser Fire over Fire | Student against the Magus | Being out-classed by a stronger or more experienced opponent | 88 |
| 2, 2, 4–6 | Greater Fire over Fire | The Dragon's Breath | Incredible energy and determina-tion, ever-increasing speed and heat | 86 |
| 2, 3, 1–3 | Lesser Fire over Water | The Nymph | Flirting, plucking at the emotions | 112 |

| Dice Roll | Elements | Title | Summary | Page |
|---|---|---|---|---|
| 2, 3, 4–6 | Greater Fire over Water | The Invincible Flame | The determination to succeed against all odds | 110 |
| 2, 4, 1–3 | Lesser Fire over Earth | Tending the Campfire | Responsible care of home comforts and security | 136 |
| 2, 4, 4–6 | Greater Fire over Earth | The Forest Ablaze | Clearing the way of obstacles, destroying the status quo | 134 |
| 2, 5, 1–3 | Lesser Fire over Sun | The Prodigy | A wise student; first steps in a new project | 160 |
| 2, 5, 4–6 | Greater Fire over Sun | The Runners | A close race, triumphing against a superior | 158 |

| Dice Roll | Elements | Title | Summary | Page |
|-----------|----------|-------|---------|------|
| 2, 6, 1–3 | Lesser Fire over Moon | The Mantra | A light to guide the way toward mysteries, repetition | 184 |
| 2, 6, 4–6 | Greater Fire over Moon | The Shout | Imposing your will; gathering your determination and acting | 182 |
| 3, 1, 1–3 | Lesser Water over Air | The Softening Heart | Tackling sternness and sharp control with caring emotion | 68 |
| 3, 1, 4–6 | Greater Water over Air | The Storm | Clearing the mind and washing away the previous situation | 66 |

| Dice Roll | Elements | Title | Summary | Page |
|-----------|----------|-------|---------|------|
| 3, 2, 1–3 | Lesser Water over Fire | The Diplomat | Placating another person, soothing a situation | 92 |
| 3, 2, 4–6 | Greater Water over Fire | The Rescue | Defusing a situation, adapting successfully to a threat | 90 |
| 3, 3, 1–3 | Lesser Water over Water | The Rain on the Lily Pond | Emotions nurtured, gentle happiness and refreshment | 116 |
| 3, 3, 4–6 | Greater Water over Water | The Dreaming Sea | Mastery of dreams, careful steering of deep tides | 114 |
| 3, 4, 1–3 | Lesser Water over Earth | The Rains | Happiness and good fortune; the crops are watered | 140 |

| Dice Roll | Elements | Title | Summary | Page |
|---|---|---|---|---|
| 3, 4, 4–6 | Greater Water over Earth | The Deluge | Emotion and vision triumph over blockages, healing replaces stasis | 138 |
| 3, 5, 1–3 | Lesser Water over Sun | The Rainbow | Positive emotions, caring and supportive attitude | 164 |
| 3, 5, 4–6 | Greater Water over Sun | The Dream Master | Powerful control of your emotions and imagination | 162 |
| 3, 6, 1–3 | Lesser Water over Moon | The Silvered Dish | Simplicity, silence, divination; calm action to see the truth | 188 |
| 3, 6, 4–6 | Greater Water over Moon | Treasure in the Depths | Yearning for something out of reach, powerlessness | 186 |

| Dice Roll | Elements | Title | Summary | Page |
|---|---|---|---|---|
| 4, 1, 1–3 | Lesser Earth over Air | The Tentative Step | Not rushing to make thought into reality | 72 |
| 4, 1, 4–6 | Greater Earth over Air | The Overworked Scribe | Ideas taking physical form, daily demands interfering with plans | 70 |
| 4, 2, 1–3 | Lesser Earth over Fire | Wood for the Fire Pit | Careful fueling bringing order | 96 |
| 4, 2, 4–6 | Greater Earth over Fire | The Treasury-Keeper | Preventing danger by having sensible plans, creating order and wealth | 94 |
| 4, 3, 1–3 | Lesser Earth over Water | Quicksand | Out-of-control emotions not grounded enough | 120 |

| Dice Roll | Elements | Title | Summary | Page |
|---|---|---|---|---|
| 4, 3, 4–6 | Greater Earth over Water | The Reservoir | A fortunate supply of help, nourishing roots | 118 |
| 4, 4, 1–3 | Lesser Earth over Earth | The Ploughed Fields | Strong beginnings; hidden stability, good foundations | 144 |
| 4, 4, 4–6 | Greater Earth over Earth | The Mountain | Protection and resilience, a safe fortress | 142 |
| 4, 5, 1–3 | Lesser Earth over Sun | Discarding the Mask | Recognition for your achievements | 168 |
| 4, 5, 4–6 | Greater Earth over Sun | The Farmer | A hero hidden by normality, success by mundane means | 166 |

| Dice Roll | Elements | Title | Summary | Page |
|---|---|---|---|---|
| 4, 6, 1–3 | Lesser Earth over Moon | The Waking Dreamer | A gentle return to solid ground; a lingering feeling of oddness | 192 |
| 4, 6, 4–6 | Greater Earth over Moon | The Family Meal | Grounding, recovering from instability | 190 |
| 5, 1, 1–3 | Lesser Sun over Air | The Eagle's Nest | Gentle healing, lots of space, and fresh breezes to clear the mind | 76 |
| 5, 1, 4–6 | Greater Sun over Air | Clear Summer Sky | Freedom to celebrate life and success in comfort | 74 |
| 5, 2, 1–3 | Lesser Sun over Fire | The Guildmaster | Skillful assistance from an expert source | 100 |

| Dice Roll | Elements | Title | Summary | Page |
|---|---|---|---|---|
| 5, 2, 4–6 | Greater Sun over Fire | Knighthood | Passion becomes success; recognition over your peers, glory | 98 |
| 5, 3, 1–3 | Lesser Sun over Water | Diamonds in the Stream | Glimmers of brilliance, treasures to be found | 124 |
| 5, 3, 4–6 | Greater Sun over Water | The Sunny Shore | Physical feeling, joy, health, leisure | 122 |
| 5, 4, 1–3 | Lesser Sun over Earth | The Fields at Sunset | Work still to be done, endings and choices | 148 |
| 5, 4, 4–6 | Greater Sun over Earth | The Monarch | Promotion, recognition | 146 |

| Dice Roll | Elements | Title | Summary | Page |
|-----------|----------|-------|---------|------|
| 5, 5, 1–3 | Lesser Sun over Sun | The Navigator | Small corrections to an already successful course | 172 |
| 5, 5, 4–6 | Greater Sun over Sun | The Triumphant Sun | Unmitigated success; health, vitality, rightness | 170 |
| 5, 6, 1–3 | Lesser Sun over Moon | The Attentive Spouse | A reliable partner, supportive or correct behavior, a team | 196 |
| 5, 6, 4–6 | Greater Sun over Moon | The Queen Crowned | Success in magic, control and skill | 194 |
| 6, 1, 1–3 | Lesser Moon over Air | The Touch of Silver | The rational is given a small touch of magic | 80 |

| Dice Roll | Elements | Title | Summary | Page |
|-----------|----------|-------|---------|------|
| 6, 1, 4–6 | Greater Moon over Air | The Ecstatic | Magic and mystery break through doubt and overthinking | 78 |
| 6, 2, 1–3 | Lesser Moon over Fire | Candle Magic | Success in small projects, blessings for personal needs; subtlety bearing fruit | 104 |
| 6, 2, 4–6 | Greater Moon over Fire | May Day | Primal magic, wild attraction, celebration | 102 |
| 6, 3, 1–3 | Lesser Moon over Water | The Still Soul | Inner silence, focus, and serenity | 128 |

| Dice Roll | Elements | Title | Summary | Page |
|-----------|----------|-------|---------|------|
| 6, 3, 4–6 | Greater Moon over Water | The Great Tides | Nature moving in harmony, cycles | 126 |
| 6, 4, 1–3 | Lesser Moon over Earth | The Moonlit Glade | Peace and contentment, natural magic | 152 |
| 6, 4, 4–6 | Greater Moon over Earth | The Howling Wolf | Wild freedom; ecstasy, joy, adrenaline | 150 |
| 6, 5, 1–3 | Lesser Moon over Sun | The Mirror Obscured | Reflecting in another's glory, invisibility | 176 |
| 6, 5, 4–6 | Greater Moon over Sun | The Eclipse | A powerfully magical feeling; mystery triumphs | 174 |

| Dice Roll | Elements | Title | Summary | Page |
|---|---|---|---|---|
| 6, 6, 1–3 | Lesser Moon over Moon | The Phases of the Moon | Flexibility and adaptability, constant slow change | 200 |
| 6, 6, 4–6 | Greater Moon over Moon | The Full Moon | Magical power, night, religion; success of spiritual work | 198 |

# Bibliography

Addey, Crystal. *Divination and Theurgy in Neoplatonism: Oracles of the Gods*. Abingdon, UK: Routledge, 2014.

Braekman, W. L. "Fortune-Telling by the Casting of Dice." *Studia Neophilologica*. Vol. 52 (1): 2008.

Curnow, Trevor. *The Oracles of the Ancient World: A Complete Guide*. London: Bristol Classic Press, 2004.

Johnston, Sarah Iles, and Peter T. Struck, eds. *Mantikê: Studies in Ancient Divination*. Leiden, Netherlands: Brill, 2005.

Rankine, David, and Sorita d'Este. *Practical Elemental Magick: Working the Magick of the Four Elements of Air, Fire, Water, and Earth in the Western Esoteric Traditions*. London: Avalonia, 2008.

# Acknowledgments

I'D LIKE TO thank S and D for providing solid earthy foundations and starry skies when I was first learning to shape the elements. It's only when talking to friends during the writing of this book that I realized quite how many years ago the initial parts of it were already in place.

Huge thanks to Emily, for all the help on the path to getting published.

And thank you to Elysia and Aaron for their hard work on a book with odd requirements, and making the process so easy.